A New Culture of Energy

A New Culture of Energy

BEYOND EAST AND WEST

Luce Irigaray

A New Culture of Energy has been translated by
Stephen Seely with Stephen Pluháček

The Mystery of Mary has been translated by
Luce Irigaray and Antonia Pont

Columbia University Press
New York

Columbia University Press
Publishers Since 1893
New York   Chichester, West Sussex
cup.columbia.edu

Library of Congress Cataloging-in-Publication Data
Names: Irigaray, Luce, author. | Seely, Stephen D., translator. |
Pluháček, Stephen, translator. | Pont, Antonia, translator.
Title: A new culture of energy : beyond East and West / Luce Irigaray ;
translated by Stephen Seely, Stephen Pluháček, and Antonia Pont.
Other titles: Nouvelle culture de l'énergie. English.
Description: New York : Columbia University Press, [2021] | Translation of:
Une nouvelle culture de l'énergie : par delà orient et occident.
Identifiers: LCCN 2021017832 (print) | LCCN 2021017833 (ebook) |
ISBN 9780231177122 (hardback) | ISBN 9780231177139 (trade paperback) |
ISBN 9780231551540 (ebook)
Subjects: LCSH: Mary, Blessed Virgin, Saint. | Energy medicine. |
Psychotherapy. | Yoga—Therapeutic use. | Breathing exercises—Therapeutic use. |
Spiritual healing. | Mind and body. | East and West.
Classification: LCC RZ421 .I75 2021 (print) | LCC RZ421 (ebook) |
DDC 615.8/24—dc23
LC record available at https://lccn.loc.gov/2021017832
LC ebook record available at https://lccn.loc.gov/2021017833

Columbia University Press books are printed on permanent
and durable acid-free paper.
Printed in the United States of America

Cover design: Julia Kushnirsky
Cover image: istockphoto

Contents

CONTENTS

{ I }

A New Culture
of Energy

TRANSLATED BY STEPHEN SEELY
WITH STEPHEN PLUHÁČEK

Introduction

IT WAS BY CHANCE, or rather out of necessity, that I began to practice yoga. After a car accident, I consulted an osteopath who strongly advised me to see a yoga instructor he knew to set about strengthening the muscles in my back so as to overcome the paralyzing effects that resulted from the accident.

This was how I first met François Lorin. He had just concluded a yoga class with a group of his students by explaining to them that "all can become conscious." I practiced psychoanalysis at the time, and when he approached me, asking me what I expected from him, I responded, "Nothing." He asked me to explain, and I told him, "I am a psychoanalyst, and I do not believe that everything can become conscious." His only response was: "Are you in pain?" I could only answer in the affirmative. He then suggested that I take a chance on relieving this suffering through the practice of yoga, and I agreed to try.

For years, I practiced yoga primarily while on school holiday, when I would meet François Lorin in the south of France where he lived. Most often, the teaching took the form of private lessons. One part of the meeting would be devoted to the practice of postures, another to the practice of breathing, and a third to an exchange between us that would touch upon the effect that yoga had on my health and also about the readings that François Lorin had recommended to me in order to increase my familiarity with the culture of yoga or with the experiences of the masters of this tradition.

Sometimes I complained to François Lorin that I was not progressing fast enough, saying that the practice of yoga allowed me only to live from morning until night. To which he responded that this was already not so bad. He was right. Thanks to the practice of yoga, however irregular it was, I regained the use of my partially paralyzed arms and resumed a normal life. I also began to familiarize myself with another culture and another world than those with which I have been familiar since childhood. But I was still approaching this culture and this world as a foreign reality that I was getting to know only little by little.

After ten years of practice, this culture and world had become mine and I could no longer tell if I belonged to the Western world or to the Eastern world where yoga was born. I belonged—I belong—henceforth to both. This happened imperceptibly through a practice that became a daily one and that modified the perception I had of myself as well as of the world and of others. This practice was accompanied by reading some of the major texts of the culture of yoga that recounted the experiences of practitioners as well as by the discovery of part of the artistic world produced by this tradition: sculpture, music, and even certain literary texts. I have approached the architecture above all in reproductions, having visited India only once and only to practice yoga in the ashram founded by Sri T. Krishnamacharya, in which T. K. V. Desikachar, his son and pupil, was then the principal instructor. At that time—December 1983—I also attended with great delight the music festival that took place in Madras (now Chennai). But I did not have the opportunity to visit any temples outside Madras.

In this initiation to the culture of yoga, I have been accompanied by different instructors—François Lorin, Laurence Maman, Bernard Bouanchaud—all of whom were trained by T. K. V. Desikachar in the school founded by his father and master Sri T. Krishnamacharya. Although each of these instructors revealed particular aspects of the practice and the culture of yoga to me, they all inspired me to discover and follow my own path. Out of personal necessity, I decided to become vegetarian, stop smoking, and adopt a rhythm of life that each day includes a walk, writing a poem, and a moment of meditation separate from my yoga practice. What these different teachers taught me, with more or less rigor, is that a certain discipline must be substituted for the culture of sacrifice that is so prevalent in the Judeo-Christian tradition. Whether or not they insisted on the fact that a daily practice of yoga must be part of this discipline depended on their degree of commitment to the yoga tradition.

It is the practice of yoga itself that has changed me bit by bit and imposed certain decisions on me. These decisions, in reality, deprive me of nothing but rather allow me to reach another stage in my journey—a journey in which the end is not fixed a priori, but in the course of which certain possibilities are opened and others are closed as I go on my way. Nothing whatsoever is decided or imposed from the outside by some master or doctrine: the path to be followed is determined from within myself and in fidelity to my daily experience. Occasionally there are complex dilemmas, particularly between a choice that is more Western and one that is more Eastern. And this brings me back to a question that is inescapable in our epoch given its multicultural character: what does it mean to be a human being? How can I fulfill my humanity—in relation to myself as well as in relation to nature, to the world, to the other or others, and to a possible transcendence relative to human existence?

I am far from having found the answers to these questions, and even from having yet addressed them all. What I *can* say is that they do not appear to me in an abstract, merely theoretical or moral fashion, as I so often hear them treated in debates about the right attitude to adopt in relation to one's own culture and another. Rather, it is a question each time of a global engagement, of an option implicating everything that I am and that will determine the rest of my life. It is experience that will later reveal to me whether the choice I made was the right one and not some supposed sanction—a sanction that, moreover, would be beyond my earthly existence. The effect of my decision on daily life will decide its validity.

In the culture of yoga, the first imperative is to do no harm, either to others or to oneself—an imperative that should, modestly, precede the Christian commandment to love the other as oneself. If my decision is harmful, to me or to the other, then it should be renounced. Otherwise, why not be faithful to it, remaining attentive to the benefit that it may or may not generate (a benefit that is often difficult to predict and must therefore be risked in order for the validity of the decision to be tested)?

Such a course is quite different from one marked out in advance, which is what the Western tradition usually offers us. It is no longer a question of simply complying with predefined laws or of following paths drawn independently of us; rather, it is our own experience that must instruct us, teaching us bit by bit to become our own masters. Not out of disdain for the lessons received from our tradition or ingratitude for them, but because each one of us represents an indispensable link in the becoming of humanity and because accomplishing ourselves is an essential task for all humans.

The Liberation of Energy Through Psychoanalysis

MY PSYCHOANALYTIC training and my profession as a psychoanalyst have taught me that traditional Western medicine cannot cure everything. If physical pain has a psychic origin, then no medicine can cure it. Some of them may, occasionally and momentarily, relieve the suffering. Nevertheless, there is the risk that they displace and even amplify the suffering, reminding us that the cause of the malady is still there. Recourse to a psychoanalytic cure or therapy could perhaps get rid of the symptoms where no medicine had achieved results.

In the relation with the therapist, the cause of the suffering often appears through the reactualization of past situations that have caused trauma—a trauma that was experienced blindly at the time of its occurrence and that is physically expressed for lack of being spoken and resolved at another level. For example, a familial milieu that is too authoritarian or repressive can provoke respiratory or other paralyses, an abrupt separation from the mother can engender in an infant a refusal to eat that can later take various forms, and a paternal absence can be the cause of a difficulty in distancing oneself from the first human bond that affects the ability to orient oneself and take suitable initiatives in a social context.

Psychoanalytic work must lead the patient to relive the traumatic situation, in particular through the actualization in the bond with the therapist of what caused the trauma. This is in fact the only way to make the patient truly conscious of a trauma, which is always alive and active, and that provokes symptoms, especially physical ones, without a detectable reason or possible treatment. It is when the therapist becomes the repressive father or mother, the vanished mother or the absent father, that the patient can—by suffering from the relation that has been created with the therapist—finally arrive at an understanding of the origin of the suffering and discover how to overcome the trauma that he or she has endured. This certainly cannot happen by denying the origin of patients' suffering: the trauma existed and in a sense cannot be effaced. However, knowing the source of his or her suffering, the patient can, with the aid of the therapist, take on the trauma and discover how to arrange his or her life so that this trauma will no longer obscurely hinder his or her existence, especially through physical symptoms.

For many practitioners, the basic scenario of a psychoanalytic cure unfolds primarily at the level of discourse. At best, the patient then relives the traumatic situation, and the psychoanalyst puts, or helps to put, what happens, what the patient experiences, into words. I have rarely acted in this manner. I have instead paid attention to the energetic configuration that has been put in place and have attempted to make it evolve while avoiding naming anything, so as not to risk paralyzing energy once again in or with words. I have not tried to undo the trauma by designating it, and in a certain sense duplicating it, with words. I have tried to liberate energy otherwise. For example, when the patient projected onto me a certain role, a certain fantasy, or a certain image, I did not necessarily say anything about this but instead tried to fulfill another function in order to break the deadlock in the situation and restore mobility to the energy.

I have often resorted to such a method by using the patient's own language. In his or her way of speaking, each person expresses the relational configuration in which he or she is situated. This is true with regard to the difference between the sexes but also with regard to the neurosis or psychosis from which the patient suffers. The question is not necessarily one of the words that are used, but rather of the way in which he or she connects them. And it is particularly interesting to note how a subject utilizes the words that have a relational function in discourse—for example, pronouns: *I, you, he/she, we, you* (plural), *they*; but also prepositions: *with, to, for*; or adverbs: *together, at the same time*, and so on. The type of verbs that the subject employs is also very revealing. The use of certain verbs implies the possibility of a more or less reciprocal relation with the other—to greet (one another), to speak (to each other), to meet (one another), and so on—whereas certain other verbs instead privilege the relation of a subject to an object—as to fabricate, to employ, to use, to consume—and still others express a quite solitary autonomous activity—as to walk, to draw, to create. The way in which the tense—past, present, or future—or the moods—indicative, imperative, subjunctive, infinitive—are utilized is equally very significant. These are only a few indications of the way in which the energetic life of the subject is conveyed in his or her language.

Aware of a reality that a linguistic approach and numerous studies on different types of discourse have awakened in me, it has been possible for me to modify the energetic economy of a patient in therapy by highlighting, for instance, his or her use of "you" to the detriment of "I" or vice versa, a quasi-exclusive use of the past or the future tense, the fact that he only utilizes the preposition "with" to express a subject-object relation ("I write this text with a pen") and not a subject-subject relation ("I write this text for you" or "I live with a friend," etc.). I cannot fully develop here the numerous studies, analyses, and interpretations that I have carried out on the pathology or on the sexuation of discourse. To better understand what is in question, I suggest that the reader consult some of the texts listed in the footnote.*

* See, for example, *To Speak Is Never Neutral*, trans. Gail Schwab (New York: Routledge, 2002), but also my numerous analyses of the sexuation of language in *Sexes et genres à travers les langues* (Paris: Grasset, 1990); *I Love to You: Sketch of a Possible Felicity in History*, trans. Alison Martin (New York: Routledge, 1996); and the issues of the journal *Langages*, for example, "Le sexe linguistique" (1987) and "Genres culturels et interculturels" (1993).

What I am trying to say is that my way of practicing psychoanalysis has prepared me for an approach to yoga as a therapeutic practice, even if it was a car accident that ultimately brought me to yoga. I do not believe, however, that yoga therapy can be substituted for psychoanalytic therapy, or vice versa. A yoga instructor lacks knowledge, and above all experience, of the psychic mechanisms that allow for the revival or the reminiscence of past traumas through transference, and a psychoanalyst most often has a quite poor perspective on energetic functioning, especially in its physical components. The yoga instructor and the psychoanalyst have very different competencies, which belong, moreover, to different traditions. Confusing the two risks paralyzing everything in a sterile indifferentiation at a time when we need, more than ever, a foresight that makes us able to build bridges between different cultures.

No doubt, both yoga therapy and psychoanalytic therapy have to do with an energy that they must liberate, make circulate, and learn how to cultivate. However, yoga deals more with a vital elementary energy and psychoanalysis with a more elaborated energy—a psychic energy that, as such, perhaps does not exist in the culture of yoga. Indeed, this culture does not follow the same tradition with regard to subjectivity, and it is possible that our notion of the unconscious would not make sense there. This could explain the remarks of François Lorin, who shocked me when he told his students that "everything can become conscious." This would be possible in the West only by modifying logic itself and by changing the sense of what is understood by conscious and unconscious.

At any rate, I do not see how a practice of yoga could render conscious what has been unconscious according to the Western tradition or how it could heal unconscious trauma. Yoga can help someone who suffers through a practice that restores energy to him or her, which is certainly more favorable to the whole organism than taking medicine to treat a symptom. Yet a practice of yoga cannot, for all that, undo unconscious conflicts tied to a person's past or to his or her belonging to a certain tradition. This practice then risks the negation or denial of these conflicts, leading to a negation of subjectivity itself. Moreover, it is common among yoga practitioners to focus on the observance of, not to say the submission to, a supposedly neutral technique without questioning it. Thinking is often considered contrary to yoga, which is probably due to a misunderstanding regarding the subtlety of this tradition and in order to avoid interrogating the possible or impossible cultural linkages between the Western tradition and that of yoga. This is conducive neither to the development of the personality of the practitioner nor to the relation between the traditions to which each practitioner should contribute for him- or herself, for others, and for the promotion of peace and fecundity between different cultures.

Yoga as a Road to Recovery

MY OWN JOURNEY has allowed me to experience how a regular practice of yoga can resolve certain problems created, particularly for feminine subjectivity, by the tradition in which I have been educated. Western culture has been defined above all by men in order to resolve their own needs and subjective difficulties. By failing to establish relations with the mother that take into account the existence of two human identities with different properties, especially concerning procreation, man has thought that asserting himself as man occurs through the domination of nature. The nature to be mastered was, according to him, both the natural universe itself, with which he equated the mother as a reproductive ground, and his own natural identity. Western culture represents a world in some way parallel to the natural world that it intends to dominate through the creation of a spiritual world. To be cultured, in the West, corresponds to the submission of nature by means of logical rules or technical tools that, in the end, serve necessities that are more masculine than truly human. What's more, we could add: necessities of masculine subjectivity and consciousness at a specific point in their evolution. There is hope that the affirmation of a different human subjectivity, that of woman, will be able to help man to resolve his relations to nature, to the mother, and to his own proper natural identity in a way other than through domination and subjection to his own needs and instincts.

In the meantime, it is necessary to take account of the fact that Western cultural identity, to a great extent, is constructed upon the submission of nature to rules and techniques that aim at dominating it, upon the subjection of the body to the spirit, and also upon the subjection of the feminine, which is equated with nature and the body, to the masculine, which is supposed to be the only creator and actor at the cultural and spiritual levels.

Dichotomies of this kind are not conducive to the production, circulation, and transformation of energy in each of us, or between us, in particular with regard to our differences. Indeed, if our energy arises first and foremost from an energy existing in nature and in our body, then intending to master it by logical rules or by techniques is not favorable to its production and runs the risk of sterilizing or paralyzing it. A culture in which the spirit pretends to dominate the body is a culture that cares little about the preservation and transformation of our energy in order to pass from a natural identity to a cultural or spiritual identity. This transforms us into all sorts of automatons rather than into cultivated living beings. The automaton functions from an artificial source of energy that is external to it and not from the energy that it could produce as a living being. The submission of our natural energy to logic and techniques that are foreign to it has rendered this energy in some way artificial, and it therefore functions in accordance with mechanisms that are no longer those of our nature. These mechanisms amount, for example, to cultural habits or imperatives—waking up at a certain time, going to work, behaving in this or that manner according to established codes, and so on. This does not necessarily signify a cultivation of our vital energy but rather the subjection of it to coded forms that, moreover, can vary at different times.

The pathologies from which we suffer often originate in the fact that the codes that are imposed on us and to which we must submit do not respect our natural energy. They repress it instead of allowing it to flourish thanks to its cultivation. Such a gesture requires us to transform our own natural energy into spiritual energy, which means the spiritualization of the body itself and not its submission to a spiritual model that is extraneous, even hostile, to natural life.

Doing yoga can help us recover part of our natural energy as well as increase it through a practice of appropriate postures and, above all, through a cultivation of breathing. Besides its healing power, the latter could lead us to experience what free energy is—a rather rare experience in Western tradition in which energy is immobilized in ideas, beliefs, moral imperatives, habits, norms, and stereotypes. Discovering the possibility of a free disposal of energy amounts to a path of healing for a Westerner. For him or her, the question will be to find out how to cultivate a natural energy that he or she knows only in the form of instincts, drives, or passions—more or less human, more or less pathological and reprehensible. What can be done with an energy that remains natural but is already spiritual if it results from a voluntary practice, in particular a practice of breathing?

This possibility opens up new opportunities for individual and collective becoming that traditional psychoanalysis has not sufficiently considered. For it the challenge was to release the patient's energy in order to bind it in a more adequate manner, but not to set it free so that the patient can have it at her or his disposal. It is true that the responsibility for our own energy represents a new problem for humanity, one that requires us to reach a greater maturity and to take charge of the continuation of our evolution as humans. Instead of culture being synonymous with the submission to rules, norms, or ideals defined and imposed by past generations, the task incumbent upon us would be to create a more human future thanks to the discovery of a free energy that we ourselves have to care for.

Transforming our natural energy without repressing it is particularly indispensable in the relations between us—above all, but not only, in amorous relations. Attraction, especially sexual attraction, is the

largest source of energy for humans. Repressing it instead of cultivating it deprives us of the energetic resources that we need in order
to live as humans and to share our humanity. To let sexual attraction express itself in an immediate manner without cultivating it,
however, means that energy, which has been awakened by the other,
is exercised in an instinctive way in order to possess, appropriate,
dominate, or submit oneself to this other, even to satisfy a procre-
ative instinct. Energy is then utilized and expended for lack of being
transformed into desire and love that can be shared between two
humans—a situation that itself is a source of energy.

Certainly there is in our tradition a way of transforming natural energy into cultural energy, but this often occurs through subjecting it, and even sacrificing it, to ideas or ideals that are abstract
and supposedly neuter. One would then agree to renounce a sexual
attraction for the other in order to devote our desire to the Other or
to a moral, cultural, or political ideal. This often leaves us divided
between unsatisfied natural instincts and desires for an unattainable
Absolute. This does not encourage in any way our relations to the
other, who is subjected either to our instinct or to our ideal without
being recognized, desired, and loved as an autonomous and different
human in relation to us. This can lead to nothing but pathological
traumas on either side. Life as such is always sexuate and a human
being is a relational being who must fulfill his or her desires in order
to flourish.

Too often, our culture keeps us in a state of ignorance or infancy
with respect to our desires. At best we share our needs—food, shelter, money, and so on—without reaching the stage of an adult sharing of our desires. Our culture serves as a familial tradition in which
we take shelter and which we perpetuate without taking the risk of
inventing and creating our lives according to our desires and our
epoch. Taking this risk can occur only if we are capable of acquiring
a real autonomy with respect to our family—all the forms of family that have helped us to become more or less adult humans: our
natural family, but also our cultural or religious family. To become

autonomous, then, means being capable of opening ourselves to a world different from the one already known and lived, in our own existence as well as in the encounter, including the amorous encounter, with the other. Our autonomy is a sign that we have freed our energy from traumas and paralyses and that we are capable of investing it and sharing it according to our desires.

Gaining Autonomy

THE FIRST GESTURE of autonomy that a newborn achieves is to breathe by her- or himself, a gesture that does not usually happen without anxiety or some pain. The first autonomous breath of the newborn is generally accompanied by a cry that does not seem to be a cry of joy! Before birth, the fetus receives oxygen through the blood of the mother. No doubt, the placenta provides the fetus with a certain autonomy: it regulates the vital needs of the fetus and of the mother, and makes possible their coexistence, whatever their differences may be, including that of sex.* But the autonomy made possible by the placenta in its role as third is suitable for embryonic life, not beyond.

At the elementary vital level, nature imposes its law by requiring the newborn to breathe in an autonomous manner just as he or she leaves the placenta and the mother. Unfortunately, the newborn's quasi-automatic respiration is rarely the subject of awareness and education in our Western tradition. And yet these are necessary in order to ensure the autonomy of our life as human life. If that which ensures the first autonomy of our existence is not taken into

---

* See the dialogue with the biologist Hélène Rouch, "On the Maternal Order," in *Je, Tu, Nous: Toward a Culture of Difference* (New York: Routledge, 1993).

consideration, we fall back into a prenatal dependency. The milieu in which we live, the culture or society that are ours, become, in turn, kinds of placentas in which we shelter ourselves and from which we draw, at least partially, our subsistence. But such a subsistence is no longer supplied with oxygen; it is nourished by something already fabricated, already partly dead. And this cannot maintain our own life nor permit it to develop.

Certainly, we receive breath from some already existing words inscribed in our tradition and from certain works. But we cannot simply take sustenance from them without making them ours in an autonomous way and actively contributing to carrying on this tradition ourselves. Otherwise, we utilize the life that this tradition transmits to us like the oxygen conveyed by the maternal blood and, as such, we remain, at best, at an embryonic stage—something that is problematic at the cultural or spiritual level.

We might also continue to live thanks to and through others without assuming and affirming our own existence. Then we become like parasites or cancerous cells that subsist and proliferate by feeding on the life of others, which does not allow us to become autonomous and makes any relation between us impossible.

To become aware of the fact that our life exists thanks to our own breathing is essential for making us autonomous living persons. But we cannot live only at the level of elementary vitality like an infant at the beginning of his or her existence. We must take charge of our life and transform it into a human existence. This requires us to maintain and develop our breathing and also to provide ourselves with a reserve of available breath: a soul, which enables us not to let our breathing be dependent only on the immediate necessities that are imposed upon us. Indeed, this is the first sense of the word *soul*.

With a soul we can use our breath in order to become humans, and not only to survive as living beings. The free breath of the soul must be available to us for breathing, for loving, for listening and speaking, and also for thinking in an autonomous way. Without this reserve, we lose our autonomy. But this can be maintained only by continually transforming our vital respiration into a spiritual respiration—into a breath for use in thinking, in meditating, or in praying, into a breath inspiring our words and permitting us to listen to the other, a breath making possible and sustaining a love that is desired, free, and reciprocal. Without a soul as a reserve of breath formed and preserved by each of us, all properly human activities and attitudes are impossible. They can, at best, exist as the repetition, imitation, or simulation of gestures that are not truly ours, which are therefore not the gestures of living persons present to themselves and to others.

One could say that the soul in some way ensures within us the function that air ensures outside us. And, as the plant world does for the air, we must constantly purify our inner breath of that which pollutes, paralyzes, destroys, and renders it unusable and toxic for our life and the life of others.

The external air must be pure in order to be able to protect our natural and spiritual existence, and the breath of our soul must also remain pure to permit us to attain a living and available speech and listening, a sound thought, a true and shareable love. Sometimes I use the word *virgin* to designate this state of the soul. The word, then, is endowed with a sense different from the one that is given to it in our religious tradition. It is a matter of us acquiring and keeping an autonomous and living soul rather than of keeping our body pure in an original, natural state.

Maintaining a virgin soul is possible through a cultivation of breathing, of concentration, and of meditation. It is also possible thanks to a practice of self-affection that is not in any way egoist or egocentric, and which has nothing to do with autoeroticism. Rather, it is a matter of becoming individualized and placing oneself among other living beings, whether human or not—of succeeding in being in oneself and for oneself the first dwelling in which one must stay and to which one must always return in order to safeguard and cultivate our life and to be able to share it. The perception of this first dwelling and the return to it can be accomplished through a conscious practice of breathing, through paying attention to the breath that animates us, and also thanks to certain positions: of the lips, of the eyes, of the hands. The contemplation of sculptures or images of the Buddha can help in this. To sit, motionless and silent, in a natural and predominantly vegetal environment, can also contribute to this. Such an environment nourishes and purifies the breath by bringing it directly assimilable oxygen.

In our tradition, we have been accustomed to entrusting our bodies to doctors, our souls to priests, and our minds to teachers. We have therefore remained dependent on others just as children are. Moreover, we have not gained the unity of our being, which is at once body and soul, body and mind. And yet this is the only way to ensure our autonomy and to take care of our health and our life.

The first gesture of autonomy of the newborn is to breathe by him- or herself. By paying conscious attention to our respiration, by a regular cultivation of our breathing, we can bring ourselves a new birth—not only vegetative but also spiritual. This is essential for a becoming that is really human. Such a becoming cannot be carried out in an exclusively passive way, either at the level of the body or that of the soul or the mind. We must actively contribute to the cultivation of our breath, our soul, and our mind. Being an adult human cannot be reduced to having reached a certain age or having become capable of providing oneself with one's own needs in a given environment. Being an adult human implies being able to liberate oneself from this milieu as one liberates oneself from the family, not to merely leave them behind, not to ensure in turn some of their needs but to bring to them, to bring to humanity, a spiritual contribution that participates in their evolution. We must not remain cultural parasites, no more than we can survive thanks to the breath that others transmit to us. To reach adulthood we must work for the accomplishment of humanity by accomplishing the unique being that we are at a given moment and place in human history.

Humanizing Our Breath

MANY OF THE people I have asked about their practice of yoga consider this practice to be useful for staying in shape and being competent in their work. For a great number of yoga instructors, yoga represents merely an interesting way of earning a living. Some Indians have even mocked me because I was trying to discover, through the practice of yoga, a new spiritual path. However, if this is not at stake, then to practice yoga risks rendering us automatons, slightly more effective but less spiritually cultivated than most Westerners. My comments and questions about this have often provoked smiles and even taunting, particularly during a trip to India with a group of yoga teachers who traveled to Madras (now Chennai) to attend a training course with T. K. V. Desikachar. I ended up leaving the group and the course in order to walk alone along the sea and limited myself to participating in the concerts at a music festival that fortunately was happening at the time. These activities, at least, purified and fed my breath, as did Lilian Silburn's book *The Energy of the Depths*, which I read in my hotel room. As for yoga teaching, as for sharing with the group, as for solace (I had just lost my father), and as for spiritual discovery, I must admit that this trip was quite a failure! With the exception of the group meeting with Sri T. Krishnamacharya who—what irony!—reaffirmed the importance of the difference of the sexes in the tradition of yoga. Now, this was one of the subjects that had brought upon me a fairly general condescending contempt during my stay in Madras. I welcomed with gratitude these living words, which contrasted with the technocratic ambiance, supposedly neutral and for me quite boring and deadly, of the overall course. I did not comment at all on the words of Sri T. Krishnamacharya, and nobody breathed a word about them, although they deserved some discussions about the existence of sexuate difference between us.

What I am trying to say is that, in my opinion, yoga cannot be limited to a technical apprenticeship of postures and types of breathing. I certainly do not deny the importance of the latter, but I think that it becomes meaningful only in a precise cultural context and with the spiritual or cultural stakes consciously known and freely assumed by those who practice it. Otherwise, there is the risk that an artificial respiration is substituted for a natural automatic respiration, supplying the practitioner with a kind of vital prosthesis but not, for all that, allowing the flourishing of her or his own life in what it presents as most singular and irreducible. If the practice of yoga can beneficially replace a medicine, it can also exile, in the more or less long term, those who practice it from themselves and from their culture without opening a path that helps them to place themselves between two cultures. Such intercultural bridges are still generally lacking. And it is undesirable that Western practitioners suffer too much from this lack and become, in a way, the involuntary building materials for future passages between Western and Eastern cultures. This book, and particularly the following statements that are inspired by my own experience, aim to suggest some guidelines for a cultivation of breath appropriate to a Western practitioner.

If the cultivation of breath through yoga has no other objective than expending it in everyday life, and especially in one's work, then is yoga not perpetuating what is most questionable in our tradition? It transforms us into more efficient, and especially more durable, automatons, but it does not much change the fact that we submit our life to a technique without giving it a meaning. Moreover, such a practice risks making robots of our bodies: in good working order but neutralized in their relational dimension. The stakes would then be limited to an accumulation of vitality in order to expend it, for lack of knowing how to transform it.

A similar process evokes the model that Freud proposes for masculine sexuality: an accumulation of tension, which must be released in order to return to a degree zero, or to what he calls homeostasis. Freud gives very little thought to the fact that sexual attraction is awakened by someone and that, instead of destroying it, it would be better to share this attraction with the one who aroused it. This requires us to enter into another economy of energy in which subjects are no longer automatons driven by natural or cultural imperatives that are more or less foreign to them, but one in which they assume and transform their energy with a view to a human work and, in particular, to a sharing with other humans. This no longer implies an expenditure or a cancellation of a supplement of life but rather its elaboration in order to safeguard it and increase it in a human creation.

Quite similar things could be said about breath. If I cultivate my breath only in order to expend it, then I do not contribute to a genuinely human culture. No doubt, I am productive, but of what nature is the work thereby produced? Does it truly serve my becoming and that of humanity? Does it truly serve life? Or does it exploit life without developing and cultivating it? And yet life does not belong merely to me. First, I have received it from those who engendered me, particularly from my mother, who nourished me from her own body, from her own breath. Maintaining my life is a way of giving thanks for the gift received, of respecting it and making its legacy productive. But I continue to receive life and breath from the natural world that surrounds me and with which I remain in permanent exchanges. It is therefore unjust to behave as a mere consumer toward nature, and especially with respect to the air that I breathe.

I must both preserve that which makes air breathable and cultivate my breath as human in order to participate in the general equilibrium of exchanges in the living world. As such, I cannot exploit for my benefit alone the breath of other living beings, human or nonhuman, especially in order to produce a work that destroys them.

A cultivation of breath thus requires us to take into consideration the development of our own life and that of the world that surrounds us. It does not seem possible to realize such a task with an exclusively neutral breath. Breath must be animated by our own intentions, by our own wills. It must adopt certain configurations and occupy space, including inner space, in various ways. It must also be bathed in the sunlight of our desire, our love. If our breath remains neutral and the same for anyone, if it is not individualized, then it is not really humanized. It is necessary for each person to transform his or her breath and raise it from an elementary vital breath to the subtlest mental breath, following his or her own possibilities.

But each person must also embody her or his breath, not only to make it spirit, according to the most common philosophical tendency of the Western tradition, but also to make it flesh, a flesh that can be shared. Our breath must be cultivated with a view toward sharing desire and love with respect for our differences. It must nourish and enrich our respective incarnations so that we might engender together not only natural children but also the becoming of humanity. For this most accomplished human flourishing, our breath must never sacrifice our body but instead transform it so that it becomes the mediator in the exchanges between us.

Our Body as Mediator

TAKING CHARGE OF our breathing and cultivating it can certainly be of great assistance for our life and contribute to improving our health. It can also make us more efficient at work. But do we become, for all that, more fully human? And do we not risk finding ourselves more isolated from one another? In a sense, we are more autonomous, less interdependent, but are we, as a result, in a better relation with the other and others? Certainly, the relation with the therapist, with the teacher, has helped us along our way, and we must be grateful to them for that. Nevertheless, this relationship remains a substitute for the parental relationship: it does not involve the forms of reciprocal relation that ought to exist between adult humans. It may even subject us, more than we were as children vis-à-vis our parents, to a parental substitute. Our body has developed, has become naturally adult, without us having attained the psychic or spiritual comportment of an adult.

For many animals, being an adult means being able to procure food and a territory, but above all to mate, procreate, and raise their young until they become autonomous in terms of their vital necessities. To be sure, animals sometimes behave in a manner that is wiser than humans, especially today, and humans even come to take animals for models. But to imitate the wisdom of animals does not yet testify to a human wisdom. For us, as humans, the evolution from infancy to adulthood is much longer and more complex than for most of the animal world. Alas, this evolution too often consists of submitting our nature to models that are foreign to it instead of educating it to be truly human. For example, from the first years of schooling, but already in the context of the family, children are practically forbidden to speak of the desires that they experience, especially of the desire that attracts them to another body. This crucial dimension of relational life must be silenced and repressed. And yet it is, rightly, what most interests children.

I have worked a great deal and in diverse countries, cultures, and social milieus with mixed groups of school children with the aim of making them aware of their sexuate identity and leading them to truly human relations with the other sex with respect for the particularities proper to each one. Such training aroused a great interest and enthusiasm on the part of the children who were finally allowed to speak of their desires, especially for one another, in a school setting.

Typically, sexual education is limited to teaching about the reproductive genital organs, which deeply wounds the sensitivity of children, and above all of adolescents. They want to be allowed to speak of their desires, to be informed about them, and not see them reduced to the inanimate coldness of anatomical diagrams. I have personally suffered this reduction to anatomy in some yoga classes in which the language used was often abstractly scientific or reduced to "animality" without a truly human dimension.

Yet it is, of course, at the level of the cultivation of language and of gesture that it is appropriate to treat the question of sexuality, and it is in this way that I have broached this question with children and adolescents. I did not encourage them to directly speak of their desires to one another, but to express them—in words, drawings, writings, plays, and so on—in order to be able to educate them with a view toward a human sexuate exchange. For example, if the boys demonstrated an insistent need to dominate or to be dominated by the other or, more frequently, to exclude the other from their world which consists almost exclusively of their own objects or fantasies, they were invited to develop, and in their own interests, a more relational comportment with their peers, especially ones who were different, starting with the girls in their class. If the girls, for their part, displayed toward the boys a desire that was too fusional or possessive, I suggested that they show a little more objectivity and, considering the behavior of the boys, that they invite them to do something together that would appeal to them both, instead of asking the boys simply to stay together, which will do nothing but frighten them away.

This is only one example to indicate that each boy and each girl was invited to express theself freely, and that each one was then taught how to modify his or her own tendencies in order to be able more easily to coexist and exchange with the other. After having become aware of the differences that existed between them and of their respective disadvantages, the boys (however less gifted they were in relational life) as well as the girls endeavored to make the relation between them possible and asked me to help them achieve it. All this took place in an atmosphere that was both very dynamic and friendly.

This type of instruction, alas, is lacking in our educational programs. And this is one of the main causes of the stereotypical behaviors of each gender. From the time when they are around ten years old, the boys gather to play football and the girls to talk about boys or about their clothes and makeup. These stereotypes are not only imposed on them from outside by society, they also develop for lack of a cultivation of relational life between the sexes. What also develops is violence and withdrawal. And when, at the time of puberty, the discourse on sexuality resurfaces and becomes inescapable, it reveals that violent feelings have increased in the boys and depressed feelings in the girls. For lack of having educated the relation of desire between them, they no longer know how to meet each other, and from then on, each sex suffers from the pathology that most conforms to their tendencies. This is the quite sad result of an educational model that has cut itself off from a crucial dimension of human flourishing!

What about yoga? One might normally expect from these circles that a special attention is paid to the sexuate dimension of the individual, since the practice is above all a corporeal one. Surprisingly, although the practitioners of yoga mean to be tolerant and open, I have almost never heard them speaking of sexuality. No doubt, there are a few practices recommended for pregnant women, but the fact of being pregnant then largely replaces the fact of being a woman. And my questions about or requests for a sexuate practice have provoked laughter rather than receiving appropriate responses. I appeared as a noninitiate who did not know that the practice of yoga is necessarily neuter. Just as teachers in the Western tradition pretend that knowledge is neuter.

The living organism is, in fact, never neuter. What therefore is the effect of a neuter instruction on a living being, especially, but not only, if it is concerned directly with the body? Sexual energy is decisive for a living organism. What becomes of the latter when instruction does not take that fact into account? And what happens, moreover, to sexuality itself in subjects who have been educated—or even initiated—without this sexuality being taken into consideration? Many amusing stories circulate about the orgasmic capacities of yoga practitioners. But such remarks resemble the more or less commercial Western discourses on the production or increase of sexual pleasure by this or that technique or pharmacopeia. Is this not a perspective that favors the consumption of the body and the expenditure of energy? How does it consider the relational importance of sexuality? The mediating role of the body in the relation? The energetic resource that can provide a truly amorous carnal exchange?

A good sexual economy is necessary, not only for personal equilibrium but for the equilibrium of a group. My teaching of children and adolescents about the awareness of sexuate identity and the coexistence between the sexes was also designed to train them in citizenship with respect for differences. Such an aspect of human formation is almost completely absent in the culture of yoga that I am familiar with and likewise in Western education. And a man as esteemed as Gandhi thought that carnal abstinence was the only means of escaping the violence that accompanies sexual desire. He even tested his aptitude for nonviolence by chastely sharing his bed with a woman. Does this truly represent an ideal to which it is appropriate to aspire? Would it not be preferable to succeed in sharing carnally without violence? Would such a solution not be more fulfilling for the man as well as for the woman who shares his bed? Chastity should instead signify for each one a necessary return to the self in order to be able to share again with the other while remaining two, which means without domination or submission, without fusion or loss of identity. This is to say, as human adults who desire the most complete and fecund exchange between one another. In such an exchange, the amorous body of each one is the mediator between the two, beyond and beneath any word.

The Emphasis on Performance Is Rarely Conducive to Exchange

THE TEACHING OF YOGA, like Western education, places the emphasis first and foremost on performance and even on competition. A yoga practitioner is not actively encouraged, any more than a student educated in the West, to be aggressive, and an openly manifested aggression will even be punished. Yet the kind of education that is delivered favors, in both cases, a certain aggressiveness. Learning to do the best possible, to acquire the most skills possible, to accomplish a task only in the most perfect way possible fosters an aggressive comportment. Perhaps this is not openly exercised, but it exists given what is required of the body as well as of the mind. An activity of mastery, of accumulating knowledge or energy, and a more or less competitive activity are expected. If this does not necessarily mean being openly aggressive toward the other, it implies that one distinguishes and distances oneself from this other, not in the name of a natural difference but in the name of an acquired quantitative difference. The matter is no longer of placing oneself in relation to the other with respect for an existing qualitative difference—that between the sexes, for example—but in terms of a quantitative difference that establishes a hierarchy between subjects. Such a difference is substituted, in a more or less obvious way, for a genealogical difference: as my father or my master was bigger and stronger than

I am, I try, in turn, to become bigger and stronger than the other in order to free myself from the parental ties. It is in terms of quantity—of muscles, of breath, of knowledge, or of skills—that one's own becoming and the relations with one's supposed peers are assessed.

This is in no way favorable to exchange, which consents to being both passive and active toward the other so as to receive from him, or from her, what their differences of nature or culture can bring to us. Agreeing to stop before the other and receive something from him or her necessitates the suspension of a solitary and competitive journey. It requires a different cultivation of attention, of listening, and a different corporeal attitude. Progress is no longer evaluated merely in terms of a capacity to grasp, capture, acquire, accumulate, or reproduce as much as possible, but in terms of agreeing to question one's own path in order to consider that of the other and to venture to receive, in the exchange, another becoming. This becoming is accomplished not only by capture, mastery, or possession—including of knowledge and techniques—but is sustained, and moreover altered, by the wonder, the questioning, the welcome granted to the becoming of the other.

All perceptions are then modified. I no longer look in order to comprehend and appropriate. And it is the same for the other sensory perceptions: I perceive in order to respect the difference between what, or who, I am and what, or who, the other is, in order to contemplate and praise a reality that is not mine, in order to marvel at the richness of life in accepting my not being the whole. Perception does not become, at best, an ecstasis through a mental appropriation that annihilates the object of my perception, instead it becomes an increase of energy that can result in a kind of ecstatic instance because of the extra energy that another living being reveals and brings to me.

In fact, the perception of another living being can follow a path parallel to that indicated by Patañjali for the perception of an object, except that it is by respecting the other as such, in his or her autonomous existence, that I can reach the stage of contemplation. From then on, contemplation will increasingly involve the whole of my being and it can become all the more intense because the "object" of perception is another human. The mutual awakening and sharing of energy, which can be produced in this way, can even end in a state of enlightenment that cannot occur in the mere mental appropriation of an "object."

Although it may happen that one speaks in yoga circles of an accumulation of energy and of an energetic atmosphere resulting from group practice, I have never heard any allusion to what could happen between two subjects in a mutually shared energetic relation. During a seminar that I held, I suggested to a researcher, a yoga instructor, that she use the words "*enlightenment in two*" in order to designate such a process, which aroused a strong interest. I myself took interest in such a possibility, so seldom evoked, from personal experiences and also because it seems to me to be a path toward the blossoming of desire. This state could even accompany a carnal sharing and make a contribution to its spiritual fulfillment. It could also be lived outside any carnal sharing in the narrower sense of the word in order to cultivate and enrich the energy awakened by a mutual desire.

It is then no longer a question of a solitary performance that is more or less competitive but of an energetic state that can arise between two different individuals in an exchange that is at once active and passive and foreign to appropriation or mastery. The light that could then enlighten the one and the other has little to do with that of Western reason or of scientific knowledge as they are generally understood. These, above all, have to do with a mental operation linked to a domination of the real by the mind. The enlightenment that I am trying to evoke here is instead an illumination of the flesh, which can take place in the meeting with the other. The light then produced is nocturnal rather than diurnal; it reveals to us, in a way that is mysterious and yet irrefutable, something of ourselves and, indirectly, of the other. It brings us back to our roots, brings us into the world again in a more or less radical way according to the intensity and the authenticity of the experience.

Contrary to the values usually promoted in teaching, as much in the East (at least the Eastern teaching with which I am familiar) as in the West, what is privileged here is a surrender to nonmastery and an attention to tactile perception. The sense of touch is involved in all our sensory perceptions, but we are barely attentive to it. We want to capture, to know, to make ours through sight, hearing, and also taste, smell, and touch rather than contemplating and allowing ourselves to be moved by what we meet, by what is presented to our perceptions. Being touched is experienced, and even taught, as the opposite of being efficient. The most developed relational model is that of taking, of grasping, of entering into possession—a model that prevails in the sexual life of men. Being moved, touched, or taken would be the lot of women. And this would take place in a certain unconsciousness or a loss of consciousness. And yet, a relationship in which energy is truly mutual and shared requires each one to be both active and passive, touching and touched. In the division between activity and passivity, touching and being touched, between two subjects—especially between man and woman—no meeting of human energies is really possible, and one therefore falls back into the mechanical model of tension-discharge described by Freud, the woman being the passive pole used by the man both to accumulate and discharge an instinctive energy that is not humanly developed and with which he does not know what to do. French philosophers renowned for their ethics—such as Merleau-Ponty, Sartre, and even Levinas—still speak of sexual intercourse in such terms. From their perspective, the caress, which ought to be one of the most human gestures, serves to subjugate the other within the sexual relation, and the hand of man is then predatory, as is his gaze. For my part, I have on the contrary tried to tell how the caress is the gesture that can give us back to ourselves after a neutralization or a loss of identity in living together or in the technical universe of work. Of course, this implies that each one is both touching and touched, contemplating and contemplated, and that the caress is a sort of exchanged speech that resituates the one and the other within the intimacy of his or her flesh, which restores each to his or her life while inviting a respectful and fecund sharing of it.*

* See the text on the caress, which concludes the chapter "The Wedding Between Body and Language," in *To Be Two* (New York: Routledge, 2000).

More Than Not Harming

Loving

IN STUDYING YOGA I have learned about the importance of "do no harm." This teaching has been very precious to me, and I think that it should be so for every person educated in the Christian tradition. The great commandment of the latter tradition is love. This is certainly the most human and the most universal of ideals to be respected if it is well understood. But it is often preached as having to be, first and foremost, the love of God and subsequently the love of the neighbor beloved in God—what is more, under pain of sin—rather than as the only sentiment capable of making the humanity in us and between us flourish. Even Jesus, the supposed master of love, is not truly considered as a model of human love but as the messenger sent by the Father to save us. Therefore, it would no longer be the love between us that is capable of healing us, of redeeming us from our various imperfections, but the love that God addresses to us through his son. This kind of interpretation of the Christian message seems to me to confine humanity to a state of infancy that is necessarily dependent upon the goodwill and the great mercy of the parents, particularly the father, to whom we would be forever indebted.

I think that it would be better to teach the message of Jesus as a message of wisdom that shows us that the heart is what can unite, in us and between us, the body and the soul, the body and the mind.

It is love that enables us to incarnate our nature in a human manner. It is love that can animate our breath and elevate it from a relatively neutral, elementary, vital energy to a spiritual energy, thereby transforming it into a truly human energy, not by submitting it to more or less abstract and neutral forms or norms but by making it sharable. This implies moving beyond the love of the parent for the child or of the master for the disciple and attaining the reciprocity of love possible only between adults. Love is that for which we are responsible, in us and between us, in order to achieve our humanity. And there is probably no other possible path, at least if love is understood as the most global gesture, as the one which can most fully incarnate us.

Such a love, which is necessarily mutual, entails doing no harm. In order to reach a loving exchange, it is necessary to avoid any behavior that could harm one or the other. Mutual love demands, first, a mutual respect—not a formal respect but an absolute respect for the life and the existence of each one. The sharing of love can take place only when two beings exchange in respect for their integrity, love then occurring as a sort of flourishing that is faithful to the rootedness of each.

To do no harm means to let the other be: to leave the other to his or her path, to his or her becoming, to his or her difference, all the while respecting oneself. Such a comportment incarnates energy, individualizes it, and allows a relation between two persons.

In the teaching of yoga with which I am familiar, as in Western education, the relation between two is hardly considered a cultural problem, except as the relationship between the master and the disciple that is substituted for the relation between the father and the son. But even in this relation the dual character serves a pedagogical purpose. The master trains the disciple to enter into the cultural heritage that is his, a heritage shared by the other disciples; the father of the family, for his part, teaches his children to be faithful to his own values. The figure of the master or that of the father is, moreover, taken over by that of the instructor or the professor, by that of the head of a political or religious family, or even by God himself. The dual relation is thus only a step toward the entry into a group, a community.

The grammatical case of the dual—which existed at the origin of Western culture in the Greek language—has disappeared little by little in our tradition, as have other words or grammatical forms that could express a relation between two different unities: the hands, the eyes, the lips, but also the sexes. What enabled the expression of a relation between two, and especially a reciprocal touching, has been eliminated from the culture. At the same time the grammatical form called the middle voice also disappeared, a form indicating a state at once active and passive, a form that is necessary in order to express our affects and share them with the other while respecting the two identities. Being two, being as two, then, has fallen back into the status of a natural bond that is excluded from the cultivated world.

Yet it is precisely in the relation between two that the passage from the natural to the cultural must first be elaborated, beginning with the relation between the sexes in which the passage from animality to humanity is played out. To neglect, or indeed to forget, the cultivation of the relation between two sexuate individuals for the benefit of the relation between a more or less neuter individual and the group amounts to rendering a cultivation of the affect between us, and also a cultivation of the difference between us, impossible. A radical harm exists at the root of such a tradition, and the principle "do no harm" then keeps a partially formal and neutral sense, even though it can take concrete forms. For example, a father can intend to give his daughter an education equal to that of his son without realizing that, in this, she risks losing her feminine identity. Or a mother, claiming to protect her son from every hardship, can make him impotent. As for spouses or lovers, for lack of having been trained to recognize and respect their differences, they run the risk of becoming unsatisfied and unhappy, each one bringing to the other what he or she, and not the other, desires.

Doing no harm is therefore a gesture preliminary to love. But if this precept remains general and neutral, it can become an obstacle to love. Like certain Western moral precepts, it is then applied without sufficient care for the reality of the other. In order to do no harm to the other, it is necessary first to be attentive to who this other is and to agree to put one's own precepts or moral values into question so as to discover what choice will not harm the other—nor, for that matter, oneself—in that which each one really is. In fact, to do no harm already implies a form of love, which must endeavor not to harm in order to be a real love.

The mix of cultures, which is now part of our daily life, makes the necessity of respecting the difference of the other in order not to harm him or her all the more apparent. This necessity exists already, and first of all, between the sexes, but what is closest to us often remains the most imperceptible. It is through the way in which different cultures treat sexuate difference that we become attentive today to the problems posed by a reality that was familiar to us. We discover that what is closest to us is also most foreign, most distant, because we have not perceived it in its difference. We have projected ourselves into and onto the other without recognizing him, or her, for what or who he, or she, is. Doing no harm requires us to take a step further in our human becoming—a step toward more recognition and love of the other as different from us.

Compassion

The Basis of a Universal Sharing

COMPASSION IS THE best known model of love in the yoga tradition with which I am familiar. Achieving compassion is certainly a great thing if such a feeling is experienced with all of our being and not in a somewhat paternalistic and condescending manner, as in the case of a superior toward an inferior, the rich toward the poor. This understanding of the word *compassion* is, alas, very common, at least in the West. And it is often accompanied by gestures that aim to abolish what is experienced by means of charity in one form or another. And yet the most loving dimension of compassion, its first and etymological meaning, is "to feel with the other." The human incarnation of Jesus represents a model of compassion in the sense that, in order to be able to love humankind, Jesus assumes a human identity because he can sym-pathize only by doing so.

To sym-pathize is to let oneself be affected by what the other feels. It is astonishing that compassion is usually spoken of only in terms of suffering and that this word, or another, does not express an experience of the other's feelings different from pain: for example, to experience their joy, their aesthetic emotion, their amorous state.

Perhaps the sense that we give to the word *compassion* always retains a too exclusively mental and hierarchical connotation. Those who sym-pathize would necessarily be more advanced on the path, more perfect and more affluent, and would lean toward the other in virtue of an idea or an image that they would have of the other's suffering. They would not experience, with all of their being, what the other lives; they would have only a mental representation that would make them feel pity. This type of compassion falls within the genealogical model of the father and the son, of the master and the disciple, and also within the dichotomy of the mind and the body. Moreover, these two sorts of models are partially related. Certainly, the compassion of the one who is more advanced on the path is commendable and is better than all of the mythical or historical models in which the natural or spiritual father kills or castrates the son in order to guard his power—unless the son kills or castrates the father to prevail over him. The compassion of the father toward the son, and vice versa, is preferable to a rivalry to the death in order to determine which one is the representative of power or authority.

The most complete compassion, however, does not take place in such a relationship but in a situation in which two individuals are in a relation that is more horizontal than vertical. It is on this condition that compassion can really occur as a passage toward the other, on this side of or beyond any words exchanged. Obviously, I am not alluding here to an immediate and blind empathy in which I risk feeling only myself through the other. Rather, I am thinking of a capacity for perceiving the other as other and for sharing what this other lives, on this side of or beyond any word or reason.

Such a form of compassion demands a too often ignored and neglected cultivation, even an asceticism, of our sensory perceptions and feelings. Often, these are subjected to a domination by the mental and are not educated as such in view of the relation with the other. By mastering sensations or sentiments in the name of reason or of an abstract and disembodied conception of existence, we deprive ourselves of a sharing with the other, particularly the other who is different from us, which would be useful in building a new culture. I do not know the other different from me, and I cannot know this other without submitting him or her to myself. But I can experience something of them independently of any identity or similarity. Passages or bridges between us could be established by compassion, by the sharing of an experience that mysteriously unites us as humans and more generally as living beings.

Indeed, this compassion can extend from us to the animal world, and also from that world to us. There are examples of this in the life of hermits in the West, as there are in that of the Buddha. The god Vishnu, for his part, is said to have been assisted in the creation of the universe by a bird. Birds are supposed to help those who aspire to spirituality in the East as well as in the West. How could they do this if they did not experience something of the state of the person that they come to help? In order to show that these are not simple images or metaphors, I will recount a few events that I myself have experienced.* One day I was at the home of a friend who lives in an apartment very high in a tall building in Paris. I was overcome by a strong vertigo that both paralyzed me and pushed me toward the plate glass window. Fortunately this friend had a cat, and it intervened by walking between the window and me until my vertigo subsided. Another example: after separating from a life companion, I no longer dared to return alone to the hermitage that I have in the forest. Mysteriously, animals have helped me do this. The morning after the first night that I managed to sleep again in this house, when I opened the shutter of my room I saw, on the grounds surrounding the house, a rabbit—or the descendant of a rabbit—who had earlier shared my life and who had escaped from the house of the neighbors to whom I had entrusted it during a trip. I felt a great joy and a great comfort when I saw this. By the time that I had dressed, the rabbit had disappeared. It had accomplished its mission: to come to welcome me. Many times, as soon as I reached the house, a bird whistled in such a human manner that I would turn to see who was greeting me in this way. This

---

* For other examples, see "Animal Compassion" in *Animal Philosophy* (New York: Continuum, 2004).

bird also signified to me that I could peacefully return to my house, that I was not there alone. For my part, I remember having helped an old dog who was almost dying by allowing the dog to have a share in my yoga practice. The animal had perceived my breathing from the other side of the house of the friend with whom I was staying; being unable to see me, the dog still came to lie next to me, and adopted the rhythm of my breathing. At first this irritated me because I was very tired myself, but ultimately I accepted this presence because of compassion. I find these personal stories a wonderful testimony to the universal bond that can exist thanks to compassion.

Com-passion appears as a bridge between the natural and the spiritual thanks to the attention to the other that such a state entails. Com-passion implies the renunciation of all egoism or egocentrism so as to contribute to a universal salvation. Only humans able to spiritualize and transfigure their nature—such as Buddha and Jesus, for example—are capable of a genuine compassion. And it is extraordinary to note that they communicate in this way with the entire universe in order to ensure what one might call a redemption of the world through love.

This kind of universal communion thanks to compassion is especially necessary in an epoch such as ours in which we have to both save the natural living world and establish bridges with humans belonging to diverse traditions and languages. Before and beyond any shareable speech, bonds can thus be created between all living beings, bonds that not only allow us to avoid conflicts and wars but also give us access to another mode of being in us and between us. Through a sort of amorous communion in which all living beings participate, another world is elaborated in which energy contributes to the union in diversity between all, men and women, toward the evolution, the happiness, and the fecundity of the world.

Incarnating Ourselves with the Help of Animals and Angels

THE COMPASSION OF animals toward us can help us accomplish our incarnation. Some gods in the East and some mythic figures in the West, as well as some of our fantasies or dreams, represent a human being still partially confused with the animal kingdom: one part of the human body or an entire human being is imagined in animal form. The thought of reincarnation itself could be explained from our difficulty to completely become incarnate as humans. Depending upon the stage we had reached on the journey, we would have to be reincarnated in this or that form. Attaining the perfection of our humanity would be what allowed us to escape reincarnation in one form or another or, in other words, to reach bliss or "Paradise."

The figures of Buddha and Jesus correspond to models of human fulfillment, at least in their epochs. Actually, these accomplished incarnations are exclusively masculine, and they teach us nothing about how to humanly incarnate our sexuality, and above all our sexuate difference. Sexuality still seems to be of use exclusively for reproduction and for inscribing us in a genealogy without it being questioned in terms of its importance and its cultivation in view of a human sharing with the other sex. The perfect man would be asexuate, or he would have overcome his sexuate belonging. And yet this is not, in fact, the case because he is a man—a man still unfulfilled at the level of sexuality, a man for whom sexuality remains at a merely natural stage of mating for the purpose of reproduction. On his own, however, man cannot represent a model for all of humanity, and he cannot even succeed in becoming incarnate as man. Moreover, sexuality is a crucial dimension of relational life that can neither be ignored nor denied but must be cultivated and shared in a human manner.

A great deal of the malaise of Christians with respect to their tradition comes from the lack of a teaching concerning the human incarnation of sexuality. Without the spiritualization, the divinization, of this determinant aspect of our human becoming and the relationship between humans, the accomplishment of love is impossible. And yet such is the very message of Jesus, along with the fact that he announces the possibility of the union between human nature and divine nature through incarnation itself. This "Gospel" should invite us to divinize our humanity and not to deprive it of a dimension of our energy that is indispensable for our fulfillment. Neglecting the spiritualization of our sexuate identity and our sexuate relations makes us regress to an impulsiveness worse than animal, one in which the human character would be, at best, perversity or the transposition of the sexual instinct into an instinct of domination or of submission, of possession, and so on.

It is amusing to note the number of cultural programs that are devoted today to animal sexuality as if, for lack of finding a teaching from the gods, or from God, humans searched for it henceforth, or anew, from animals. And it is true that their courtship displays, the tenderness between some of them in mating, might sometimes encourage humans to better embody the part of themselves that has been left in the dark by our culture. But a human being is not an animal. If we can find directions, and even assistance, from the sexuality of animals with a view to our own incarnation of sexuality, it is up to us to discover and to accomplish our human specificity. And the assistance that the animal world can provide us can represent only a step toward the accomplishment of our own incarnation.

In addition to animals, angels also appear in the Western tradition as offering assistance on the human journey. But these angels are only spiritual creatures, and they generally serve as messengers between God and humans without teaching humans how to enter into communication with one another, especially at the sexual level.

Certainly, if we had developed a theory and a practice regarding the chakras, we would be able to think that the help of animals concerns the chakras of elementary vitality and that of angels concerns the chakras related to its spiritualization. For example, in the iconography of the Annunciation it is clearly indicated that the relations between the angel Gabriel and Mary are situated at the level of the chakra uniting the breath to the heart, to listening and speaking. The announcement of the angel awakens in Mary breath at a superior level, thereby inviting her to give birth without for all that being reduced to a womb capable of carrying a child. The angel calls Mary to give birth with her own breath, her own heart, her own listening and speech—Mary listens to the angel and speaks to him—and not only with a female body capable of giving birth. The angel helps Mary to pass from the chakras that the woman, in a sense, shares with the animal world to the chakras that give to her access to the fulfillment of her humanity. Alas, instead of interpreting the mediation of the angel as that which permits the union of the natural and the spiritual, of the human and the divine within Mary herself, our tradition has too often understood it as a demand made in the name of God for Mary to renounce her humanity so as to bring forth a son for him. Which, in fact, does not make much sense. Mary can give birth to a divine son only if she herself has divinized her humanity. To imagine that God would ask Mary to renounce herself in order to give birth to a son for him is to have a strange idea of God. This understanding is nevertheless very prevalent and makes God a denigrator of his own creation rather than a redeemer of humanity. A redemption can take place only through the union of the chakras in us thanks to a transformation of our energy.

The understanding that we have of the Annunciation, and of redemption more generally, results from a lack of considering the importance of our sexuate identity and of its spiritualization in the achievement of our humanity. But does such an understanding not make us fall back into the sin that, according to the myth of the Garden of Eden, is at the origin of our tradition: wanting to be divine before even fulfilling our humanity? Certainly, in one case, the woman would actively seek to appropriate the knowledge of God, and in the other, she would submit blindly, body and soul, to his word. But in neither of these alternatives would she spiritualize her own nature with a view toward a becoming and a sharing, both human and divine, with man.

A mystery nevertheless remains in this iconography of the Annunciation and in Christian theology more generally: the figuration of the third age of this tradition, that of the Kingdom of the Spirit, by a bird. Just as a bird helps the aspirant to spiritual life in the Eastern tradition, it would be a bird that would introduce us to the third moment of our own spiritual becoming. The song of the bird would help us transform our energy without subjecting it to a discourse, to a logic that does not respect its carnal character and cannot be shared by those who do not speak the same language. The bird would guide us toward a human incarnation that we do not yet know, that we cannot imagine, but to which its song would initiate us little by little. The angel would be a figure closer to the human being than the bird. An angel would share some properties of the bird, but the angel would speak and so would fix energy instead of transforming it little by little by a song.

Do the chanted mantras try to take over the power of the bird? If these mantras repeat the different levels of vocalization of the birdsong, they are not for all that devoid of sense, a sense that is already extraneous to the bird's hymn to the light or to the amorous appeals that birds address to one another. Having become a sort of repetitive exercise based on a technique, the chanting of the mantra loses the moving character of the birdsong, which is a song of praise in harmony with the breath of the universe capable of helping us transform our natural energy into spiritual energy without submitting it to a more or less neutral technique that is extraneous to carnal awakening.

Arriving at Speech by Way of Silence

IN THE WEST, the end of a human journey amounts to the ability to gather in oneself the totality of discourses, whereas in the East, it is instead the ability to attain silence. Hegel would, on this point, be opposed to Buddha. Combining in oneself Western and Eastern cultures results in giving another value to both speech and silence and keeping them united rather than opposing them.

If the speech I utter is not rooted in a silence of which I am capable, then it is never my own speech. It repeats discourses read or heard, either directly as such or by composing an apparently new discourse from them. But the words that I speak and their organization in discourse can have a sense only by starting from my return to a silence in which I consciously choose them and freely compose them in statements or messages. In fact, very few people truly speak. They emit words that we know and thus we give meaning to what they say, but this does not mean that they really say something to us. Certainly, at the level of needs, this absence of personal sense is not always perceptible. If someone asks me for a piece of bread or a glass of water, I can understand the message that is thereby addressed to me. But this elementary level of understanding does not tell me much about who the other is and how to exchange between us as humans.

The relation at the level of needs can remain at a purely natural stage or be provided by robots. Exchange between humans takes place in a relation of being and of desire, which requires another use of speech. I cannot content myself with speaking to the other in words whose sense I have found only in a dictionary. The speech that I address to this other must find its meaning in me and in my intention of establishing a certain relation with him, or with her. I must be present in what I say and also try to be present to the other. This gesture is impossible if I do not regularly return to a silence in which I find myself again through gathering together all that I am. In this case, it is not a question of gathering myself around a theme but rather of a gathering of myself, which requires silence. Silence is the medium thanks to which I can attempt to return to the source of my being by again coming into touch with myself.

It is sometimes easier to return to silence in nature. Certainly nature is not absolutely silent, but what is heard there corresponds to the murmur of life itself—the sound of the wind, the buzzing of insects, and so on—and not to the noises that result from the organization of life in a more or less artificial way—language, the noise of machines, and so on.

Gathering oneself together in silence is indispensable in order to choose the sense that one wishes to give to one's speech but also in order to put into perspective the sense of the discourse that one hears. In order to decide on the sense that I will retain of this or that discourse—political, cultural, or religious—it is necessary that I listen to them against a background of silence and not in an interweaving of pieces of information that impose themselves on me and hold me captive without my being able to decide on the sense that I will give to them in my life. To come into the world amounts to entering into a network of cultural, religious, and political givens from which I must try to distance myself through a practice of silence so as to be able to construct, as freely as possible, my own world—which is important for being able to enter into relation with the world of the other.

Silence must also intervene between the other and me as a place in which we can meet, whatever our differences may be. Silence is the first word of welcome to the other. It is the sign that I give to this other of my being available to welcome the other as they are, without subjecting them to my own discourse, without incorporating them into my own world. Keeping silent in the face of the other is a way of recognizing him or her as other, of showing my capacity for respecting them as who they are without imposing my own norms or habits on them.

My silence is a way of saying to the other that I do not pretend to know him or her, that I offer to him or her a space in which to exist, in which to manifest his or her difference as something that is unknown to me but that I agree to welcome. My silence is a way of expressing that I do not know everything—as a father or a master is supposed to hold the truth that befits the son or the disciple—and that I am available for hearing from the other a truth that is their own, and that I encourage them to live, to cultivate, and to express without subjecting it to mine.

Obviously, such a silence is in no way a privation of words, nor is it a reticent or even hostile attitude. Instead, it represents a supplement to my world that I offer to the other so that he or she can exist there as other with respect to me.

The practice of such silence is especially necessary in a multicultural epoch such as ours. It is what might allow for the passage between different cultures without the subordination or the integration of one to the other. Our ability not to confine ourselves to our own language is the first gesture of hospitality toward the other. And this restraint with respect to our linguistic habits must be extended to the other relational gestures to which we are accustomed. For example, greeting the other is not expressed with the same gestures in every culture, and our way of acting might shock the other, whatever our intention may be. To welcome the other with respect for his or her difference(s) needs a withdrawal, a silence, a space-time that is virgin with respect to the modes of being and acting that are ours.

Silence is necessary for our own becoming in order to allow for an activity outside ourselves, but it is also for a return to ourselves, in ourselves. It is also essential for entering into relation with the other as other. And, in the end, it is possible that the capacity for being quiet and for keeping silent would be a gesture more human than that of speaking.

Contrary to what is most often said, silence corresponds neither to a void nor to death, but it is the guardian of the integrity of being, of the plenitude of life. We must nevertheless speak, but all speech is always partial compared with what or who we are. It expresses us only partially, particularly to the other. Speaking amounts to assuming a certain finitude, to accepting a partial and fragmentary incarnation—which involves suffering and is also a source of misunderstandings. The words that I speak in the present cannot express all that I am. And, for one who is conscious of it, this fact is a source of pain. All the more so since the words that I use are already coded, defined by and for others different from me, and it is thus difficult to make my singularity heard through them. Using them, I become a sort of "somebody" among others speaking the same language. Certainly, I then participate in a cultural group, but only at the price of losing part of my identity and of communicating only partially with the other.

The multiplicity of subjects in a linguistic community requires each to sacrifice, in the abstraction of the general, something of his or her life, of his or her flesh—a flesh to which it would be important that speech remain tied. To pay attention to the link between speaking and breathing can contribute to that by keeping speech alive in our own way of expressing ourselves as well as in the relation with the other, a relation in which an equilibrium between listening and speaking must be observed so as to permit each one to alternate between inspiration and expiration.

It is equally desirable to attend to the sensible qualities of speech, be it the tone of the voice, the rhythm of discourse, the semantic and phonic choice of words. Choosing verbs that favor the relation between two subjects without a possible reduction of one to the object of the other also encourages the living and dynamic character of relational energy. Avoiding any appropriation, assimilation, or seduction of the other to me, as well as attempting to cultivate intimacy without submitting it to familiarity, that is, to a world that is my own and in which the other as other has no part, are other ways of cultivating our relational belonging.

Paying attention to all the qualities of a truly shareable speech prevents us from forgetting that such a speech can arise only from a silence and can communicate something of it, without ever pretending to say what is felt in too immediate a fashion, which most often makes it violent toward the other.

The Spiritual Path Opened by Sensory Perceptions

BETWEEN SPEECH and silence, our sense perceptions are a means of exchanging with nature, with the world, and with the other. They also represent a means of cultivating our body while respecting it as a body.

In Western culture, sensory perceptions are considered to be inferior to mental activity and are to be subordinated to it. Moreover, they are often spoken of in generic terms that designate what is perceived without the subject lingering on the object of perception. Most Westerners look at trees, listen to music, enjoy a meal or a scent, rather than lingering to contemplate a birch tree, to savor an impromptu by Schubert, to taste the flavor of a peach, to breathe in the fragrance of a pine forest under the summer sun. Sense perception is then already dependent upon a mental abstraction that has separated it from its rootedness and from its living and corporeal qualities. It has therefore lost most of its value, especially its capacity to create bridges between the corporeal and the spiritual. It is by stopping in the present in its concrete singularity, in its sensible qualities, and by avoiding the substitution of a name that abstractly evokes it in its absence, that the perception of the object can lead us to pass from the material to the spiritual. Lingering to look at a daisy or a rose can help me reach a concentration to which the utilization of a large number of words and discourse is not conducive. All the sensory qualities of the flower awaken in me an attention that is situated at different levels that these qualities combine without my even knowing it. It is my whole being that, little by little, is gathered together in this way and, imperceptibly, passes from concentration to contemplation. If I take time to live this state, it is transformed into a culmination of energy that can lead to a form of ecstasy.

Such a process is described by Patañjali in the *Yoga Sūtras*. But it seems to me that for Patañjali this energetic state results from an internalization of the object that is, in fact, mental. To reach *samadhi*, Patañjali would need to abolish the subject-object duality. Personally, I believe that this state is achieved instead by maintaining the duality between the flower and myself, but by changing my way of perceiving it. I no longer contemplate it only in what is visible but also in what is invisible: the sap that animates it starting from which it appears to me without my ever being able to appropriate it either physically or mentally. It is the irreducible duality between the flower and me that leads me to a *samadhi* henceforth based in a love of life itself.

This way of reaching a state of *samadhi* is even more necessary when perception concerns another human, especially a human who is different from me. By lingering to perceive the other at a sensory level—to look at them, to listen to their voice, to touch them, etc.—it is possible for me to arrive at a concentration of my energy that can become contemplation if I respect the other as other. And the contemplative state that I experience can be transformed into *samadhi* if I pass, for example, from the visible to the invisible, from the audible to the inaudible, from the touchable to the untouchable of this other. I could say: if I pass from what is most immediately perceptible of him, or her, to what constitutes the irreducible core of his or her life and of his or her subjectivity—a core that I cannot perceive without changing my relation to perception.

In this way I can contemplate and know ecstasy in the relation to the other without for all that actively and materially seeing, hearing, and touching that which he or she is. I am affected, even touched, by a reality that I cannot appropriate in any way, but to which sense perception leads me. In my opinion, it is the recognition of an insurmountable duality between another living being—especially another human—and myself that can transform my sense perceptions into a path toward the spiritualization of my entire being without destroying their sensory character. This character has been transformed but not abolished, and it contributes to the spiritualization of my incarnation in a way that is at once corporeal and mental, individual and collective.

Indeed, by transforming my perception of the other in its corporeal aspect into a perception of the breath, the soul, or the spirit that animate this body, not only do I pass from a partial perception of the other to a holistic perception of who he, or she, is, but I also unify myself. This unification gathers my energy at a level other than that of concentration, and even contemplation, with which the perception of a visible form can provide me (cf. in this regard Gestalt theories). And my energetic state can culminate in *samadhi*, a sort of ecstasis that does not remove me from myself—as might happen in the rapture experienced by mystics in the Western tradition—but, on the contrary, brings me back to the heart of myself and makes me intensely live this core of my being which is most often imperceptible to me. Such a state, moreover, can be shared between two humans capable of the same attitude in the perception of the other. And this sharing increases the energy of each one.

Far from drawing me out of my most essential being, sensory perceptions are capable of returning me to it if their spiritual, and particularly their relational, potential is cultivated.

This is especially important at the level of touch. This sense is involved in all our perceptions: visual, auditory, olfactory, gustative, and tactile in the strict sense of the word. Yet, we do not perceive that we are touched by something that does not necessarily become visible, audible, etc. to us as such. We often know this element, which takes part in all of our perceptions, only through science and we tend to neglect it. Only when we can seize or grasp with our hands do we remember that touch exists. But then we have already been touched by many things without noticing it. Moreover, we neglect to cultivate the spiritual aspect of tactile touching. We touch living beings, especially another human, without really concerning ourselves with the decisive nature of this gesture. Touching the other—or being touched by the other—crosses the boundaries of the world in which each one lives. We do not live merely within the limits of a body, but within those of a world built from our physical, but also psychic and cultural, belonging, as well as from our individual and collective history, etc. To touch someone means to enter into this world and to risk undoing its conscious, but also unconscious, development. In fact, no touch between us ought to take place without preparation, without permission. But the relation between two worlds is so complex that we often reduce it to a relation of domination or submission of one world with respect to the other.

Moreover, it is generally in such terms that philosophers renowned for the ethical dimension of their discourse—for example Merleau-Ponty, Sartre, and even Levinas—speak of touching in the gesture of the caress. This would involve, especially on the part of man, inducing a loss of consciousness in the other, removing the other from himself, and especially from herself, in order to dominate this other and possess him or her. Touching would not serve to approach the other in order to allow a meeting, or even a union, between two subjects, but rather to annul one of the subjects, to reduce it to an object for the other. It is understandable why such a conception of the carnal relation fails to rouse the enthusiasm of spiritual leaders and why it ends in a sentiment of the *petite mort* on the part of man, to say nothing of the frustration on the part of woman.

The touch between us ought to be considered a means of approaching one another in that which corresponds to our most singular and intimate being, to a dimension of ourselves that we can neither live nor share in common everyday existence. The touch ought to be what gives each of us back to ourselves before any union between us. It ought to be a manner of wrapping us again in our singularity, in our own world, which are often lost or forgotten in the neutral or neuter character of the world of work, or in our immersion in a collective life that is poorly differentiated.

The caress, for example, ought to be what restores each one of us in our integrity, our virginity, and thus enables an "I" to be with a "you," without one and the other being assimilated to more or less neuter elements of a collective "one." The caress ought to give back to each one his or her identity instead of leading to its loss so as to eventually take possession of it. Moreover, the caress touches the skin, one of the bodily organs that is most tied to the brain, and can, through its awakening, ensure a privileged link between body and soul, matter and spirit. The caress is, or ought to be, the speech between us that, more than any other, helps us to spiritualize and to share our energy.

A cultivation of our sensory perceptions can give back to our lives—too hectic and robotic today—a rhythm that is more appropriate to the fulfillment of our incarnation and to the relations between us. Many humans sacrifice their existence more and more to an acceleration that uselessly competes with the efficiency of machines, coupled moreover with the concern for profit. Giving ourselves time to cultivate our sensory perceptions is a good means of rediscovering a rhythm that is more appropriate to our entire human identity, a rhythm that makes it possible for us to meet and exchange between us in a loving, fecund, and happy way.

Unity and Duality

BY ANALYZING THE origin of Western logic—especially through the study of cosmogonic myths, pre-Socratic philosophers, and Greek tragedies—it is possible to see how a certain dualism has been created that permits the masculine subject to differentiate himself little by little from the mother-nature. In order to emerge from the natural world, and from the maternal world that is assimilated to it, Greek man defined pairs of opposites through which he tried to master the world. These opposites were initially quite connected to natural experience—day and night, hot and cold, dry and wet, for example—and they became increasingly abstract with respect to sensory experience—good and bad, mind and body, true and false, and so on. In this way, man progressively established categories through which to apprehend and dominate the world without losing himself in it. By accentuating the opposition between the poles of a natural contrast—for example, day and night—man caused things, which are rarely situated at one pole or the other, to be deprived of their real existence: there are degrees between day and night, which means that one is never simply opposed to the other. Moreover, in such logic, the two poles rarely have the same value: one is considered more positively and the other more negatively.

By founding such categories, a little like one builds a scaffolding in order to be protected from the void of an abyss, man has divided himself in two, with one part of himself supposedly better than the other. He has moved away from a natural belonging which both is one and includes diversity: being a man with different corporeal elements, different energetic levels, different spiritual qualities. He became body and soul, or body and mind, for example, with the soul or the mind being supposedly superior to the body and having to dominate it. The battle that man has fought to differentiate himself from nature and the maternal world has become a battle within himself in which the opposing poles clash.

Faced with this dualism, it is easy to understand that man has only one desire: to reach unity. But how can this be attained without falling back into the undifferentiated unity that he has formed with the maternal world, a unity that he never truly surpassed and that no authority or paternal law really help him overcome? Certainly, Western culture has proposed, even imposed, a reversal of roles and has also put the beginning at the end. It would thus not be mother-nature who would have given birth to man, instead it would be the man-father-God who would have created woman. Our origin would therefore no longer be maternal and natural but paternal and divine.

This has not really resolved the conflict that man lives within himself between a natural and maternal part, which is supposedly imperfect, and a part created by God that ought to fight against the first part and prevail over it.

It seems that most of the oppositions between unity and duality obey the same schema in the West, but also in the East, starting from a certain moment in the evolution of logic. And all discussions between the privilege of unity or that of duality seem to unfold within a framework in which it is already a question of more or less abstract categories rather than of the real itself. Indeed, these discussions never seriously take into consideration the duality of human subjectivities—a duality that, if it is respected with all the seriousness that it deserves, permits each one to reach his or her own unity.

Of course, this unity is specific and does not correspond to a model of unity that is valid for just any human, but it is a real unity that can be lived and cultivated through the acceptance of one's difference from the other part of humanity.

It is difficult, especially for a man, to experience his unity with respect to a mother who enveloped him with her body, who nourished him with her blood. It is painful for him, in leaving the maternal world, to confront solitude. Perhaps the recognition of woman as the other part of humanity could help man to emerge from the maternal world, but without renouncing nature for all that, including his own.

Alas, the duality of the sexes is almost always already envisaged within the logic of binary oppositions aiming to surmount natural belonging. It is thus no longer a question of duality inscribed in the real itself, a duality in which man and woman represent the two unities—unities that are different but not opposed and neither of which is more valuable than the other. At least it would be this way if these two unities were considered in their respective realities and necessities instead of through a logic that is useful to the constitution of masculine subjectivity alone. It seems that this stage of individuation of sexuate identity is not yet carried out by humanity, that humanity has not yet reached its adulthood and humans remain children who are still dependent upon a maternal world, partly projected onto God.

The consequence of this incomplete evolution is that humanity remains at the material level of needs, needs that are both privileged and despised because they do not permit us to blossom in our spiritual dimension. The achievement of this part of us would remain out of reach—only a God or some entity situated beyond our earthly existence would correspond to our spiritual aspirations. And we would remain poor mortals divided between a necessarily "sinful" body and a soul or a mind waiting for their true life in the beyond. This rather schematic dualism is unfortunately at work in the majority of Western, but also Eastern, discourses dealing with human incarnation. But none of them—at least the ones that I know—seriously tackle the question of the spiritualization of the flesh thanks to the cultivation of our sexuate identity and an amorous sharing between the sexes that is a path of transforming our material body into a spiritual body.

And yet probably nothing is more spiritual in the human than desire. Nothing else so well allows us to animate our body with an energy that is not only vital but also spiritual—an energy that can permit one to be emancipated, even reborn, with respect to one's natural birth and to one's parental dependence. It is desire that frees us from the material weight of an exclusively natural body. It is desire that awakens us and elevates us to another level than that of elementary vitality. It is desire that enables us to create and not merely repeat what already exists. Desire "gives us wings," but instead of cultivating this extraordinary energetic potential we each try, at best, to awaken our energy, each for our own part, through a physical or psychic practice—when it is not aroused with various stimulants or drugs. Desire is more powerful than all of these alternative products or activities. To be convinced of this, it is sufficient to recall our first amorous emotions. But the word *desire* is hardly ever mentioned, except pejoratively, in the spiritual milieus that I know, including those of yoga. Why? Would it not be because desire exists thanks to a human duality that the most developed traditions have not considered and have not cultivated as they should? As a result, the emergence or the resurgence of desire seems to them to be a trivial reality that calls into question the learned categories of unity and duality whose function is to ensure the repression or suppression, when not the very ignoring, of desire.

All the unities or dualities defined in order to divert subjects from the first awakening of their desire leave them divided and in conflict with themselves, as well as nostalgic for a unity that they had lived obscurely in the relation with a first other, the maternal—a relation in which desire cannot truly blossom because it always remains mixed with need, dependence, and hierarchy. Nevertheless, Freud himself maintains that the wife must become a mother, and thus a surrogate mother for the husband, if marriage is to be successful. Such a theory is accompanied by a conception of sexuality that is quite poor from an energetic standpoint.

Alas, in yoga circles, the energetic resources of desire are also seldom evoked and the dual categories that are accepted and practiced here do not seem foreign to those of mind and matter that distribute the masculine and feminine roles in the Western tradition. Daring to say that the unity of each of us can be found in the respect for the duality of the sexes is out of place in these circles, and this is even suspected of wanting to debase a more or less neutral and abstract energy that technique has been able to awaken. Whatever the attention paid to the natural world, the mind is supposed to have to prevail over matter without a sufficient consideration either for the energy that each one brings to the other or for the specific way in which nature and culture are combined in man on the one hand and woman on the other.

Gods, God, or Another
Relationship to the Divine

IN CERTAIN INDIAN traditions as well as in the Greek culture at the origin of our Western tradition, it is a question of gods and not of one God, and the gods are represented as sexuate and even coupled. Their coupling is sometimes imagined as being the origin of the universe and their amorous relations as being what determines its economy depending on whether they are more or less harmonious. If the love between the gods is peaceful and happy, the cosmic world is well-balanced and even the weather is glorious; if their passions are exacerbated and experienced as chaos, the entire universe is affected and it itself suffers disruptions that could be dangerous. This relation between the loves of the gods and the cosmic order is evoked above all in India. And the god Vishnu, creator and restorer of the world, is represented with the feminine part of humanity, while the god Shiva, who corresponds to our epoch, would be the one who will save or destroy the world depending on whether his companion will be Khali or Uma Parvati—the one who inflames the fire of passions or the one who is capable of tempering them, of maintaining equilibrium, especially between fire and ice.

These divine couples, moreover, are represented without children. Unlike the later tradition, particularly the Western one, the sexuate character of the gods and their love outweigh their genealogical function. The gods are lovers rather than parents. Things seem to be inverted in the Judeo-Christian tradition in which the sex of God is effaced in favor of genealogy.

It is true that in India more emphasis is put on the engendering of the universe than on that of children, who are only one aspect of engendering. The gods Vishnu and Shiva are represented, respectively, with one foot in the water or with fire in hand according to whether they intervene at this or that moment of cosmic generation. God the Father will, as for himself, be figured with his son, and Mary with Jesus in her arms, without a divine couple appearing in this tradition. The Hindu gods embody different epochs in the evolution of life, epochs that we would have to recapitulate within ourselves in relation with the cosmos. Depending upon which stage of becoming we had reached—one might say according to the awakening of the chakra we had achieved—we would have to appeal to particular gods. The gods would be those who both show us the way and provide us their assistance without our having to pledge a total allegiance to any of them. Each one brings us something appropriate to a particular task or difficulty that we encounter.

We find something similar among the Greek gods, but they embody more human functions and attributes rather than moments in the generation or evolution of life, especially at the cosmic level, in which humanity takes part. Certainly, there are cosmogonies at the origin of the Western tradition—that of Hesiod, for example, as well as Genesis, which is part of the Judeo-Christian tradition—but here it is no longer a question of a slow germination, formation, or mutation of life in which the gods participate. The gods generally seem to inhabit a world that already exists, a world that they appropriate or divide among themselves, sometimes at the price of deadly conflicts between father and son or between brothers. The universe is no longer engendered at the rhythm of life by the love of sexuate gods but is shared between gods, now mostly masculine, and recreated by them according to their needs.

Little by little a patriarchal and phallocratic reign is established, which will impose a sociological religion to the detriment of a cosmological order of which the sexuate gods ensured the engendering and harmony. The order that is thereby established is a social order founded on rules that are foreign to the natural economy, which these rules serve to dominate and supplant both in us and outside us. Men are the creators and the rulers of this new order in which women, now the guardians of natural order, are the property of the father-king-husband and enclosed in the family residence so as not to disturb and contaminate public organization. The gods are henceforth at the service of a society of the between-men governed by more or less abstract and arbitrary laws, which are scarcely concerned with a cultivation of a love in difference that could avoid conflicts and wars. The difference between humans has become a quantitative estimation of each one's power, which no longer has any relation with a cultivation of natural identity and which often expresses an unsatisfied sexual instinct attempting to impose itself behind various masks.

Thus, at the very moment when Greek culture establishes the basis of the Western sociopolitical order, the king Creon—in the tragedy *Antigone* by Sophocles—in order to found a tyrannical power to the detriment of the hereditary royal family right, prohibits Antigone from practicing burial rites for her brother Polyneices, who died in a fratricidal combat to take over the government of the city. Yet these burial rituals are necessary so as not to disturb the cosmic order according to the matriarchal law that Creon wants to supplant. A dead person who remains without burial will not only never find rest and continue to wander but will even defile and disrupt the whole balance of the universe: the air, the sun, and also the world of living beings, especially the animal world. Creon no longer wants to respect such laws, either with regard to the entire universe or between humans themselves. If he founds a power that defies the cosmic equilibrium, he also contests the right to a love that is respectful of the natural belonging of humans, be it Antigone's respect for her maternal genealogy or her love for Haemon, her fiancé and Creon's own son. In spite of the intervention of Aphrodite, the goddess of love—another feminine figure of an epoch in which the natural order governs the relations between the world and humans, and between humans themselves—Creon condemns Antigone to be buried alive in a stone cave, to be deprived of air, of sunlight, and of the possibility of knowing love and motherhood. Both Antigone and Haemon will repeat on themselves the murderous gesture that Creon had ordered against them. The latter's wife will also kill herself. What will remain to the king is the right to exercise a tyrannical masculine authority instead of sharing an amorous, carnal, and spiritual power with the other part of humanity without scorning the natural law.

Today we are still living with the deadly and devastating effects of this seizure of a supposedly neuter power over the natural world. Alas, yoga practitioners, at least those whom I know, make little appeal to the sexuate gods of India in order to rescue the natural order, either outside us or within us. Alluding to the gods who belong to the more feminine and pre-patriarchal indigenous religions elicits knowing smiles and condescending contempt from many of them, including from the direct or indirect disciples of Sri T. Krishnamacharya for whom these gods, as well as the sexuate aspect of the culture of yoga, were so important. These practitioners prefer the cultivation of energy in the neuter to the cultivation of a sexuate identity that we have probably not yet succeeded in incarnating.

The gods who are supposed to represent the highest *chakra* for our humanity instead bear witness to an incompleteness in its achievement. Indeed, they are represented as children, adolescents, at best young men, who are still strangers to adult sexuality and to sexual sharing. When it is figured with a human form, Brahma is still a child, and Krishna and Jesus remain very young men. They do not incarnate the fullness of manhood, in either their age or their rather feminine aspect. Brahma is also imagined as a hybrid being belonging partially to the human species and partially to another kingdom, namely the vegetal. The human embodiment of Brahma would not be fulfilled, any more than that of the Judeo-Christian God of whom the theologically accepted triple figuration is a very old father, a not-fully-mature son, and a bird.

A human incarnation thus remains in suspense in the tradition of India as well as in the Judeo-Christian tradition. Claiming that the culmination of a religious journey would be to attain the neuter seems to me to be an error. Being capable of a virgin—which is not to say neuter—breath and energy must, on the contrary, help us to reach a stage of our individuation that we have not yet succeeded in incarnating, each one and between us. It is probably a matter for us of returning to some Garden of Eden and learning how to cultivate our nature and desire between us without wanting first to appropriate a knowledge—presumed to be divine—of the science of good and evil. No word exists from time immemorial that could be substituted for the words that we have to discover to speak to and love one another here and now.

A New Culture of Energy

WESTERN CULTURE DOES not really care about cultivating energy as such. It is primarily concerned with disciplining or even repressing it in children and adolescents and expending it in adults. A child who is unruly at the physical or the psychic level is considered to be in need of discipline rather than demonstrating a lot of energy, which is a valuable asset for his or her natural and spiritual life. As for an important sexual vitality in the adult, according to Freud it should be "discharged" rather than preserved in order to contribute to psychic evolution and foster relations with the other. Even sports aim to reduce energy more than arousing, conserving, and transforming it. Although they may contribute to nurturing our health by maintaining a certain somatic equilibrium, this does not yet signify care for the cultivation of energy as such or for the building of bridges between body and soul, between body and mind. In fact, traditional Western education teaches us to fix our energy through and in forms that are considered ideal and that ought to be shared by everyone without the energy of the one or the other, should it remain free, disrupting the established order. The purpose of instruction would then be to bind the energy of the child or the adolescent, even to put it to sleep, instead of awakening it to initiative and creativity—which would occur only in certain courses, such as art, well balanced and framed by others, as is the case with physical education.

There is therefore nothing surprising in the fact that during the cultural revolution of May '68 Western students, and even high school students, called for imagination to be in power. In this way they proclaimed their desire to leave behind a certain educational logic, which is not to say that they refused all authority or that they were struggling for more social justice. These misunderstandings can take place in the cultural tradition of the West, and they have too often been substituted for the true claims of the militants of '68, which instead had to do with a transformation of the energetic politics in education. Calling for more initiative in relation to culture does not mean challenging every kind of master but rather demanding that they teach differently, which does not amount to the same thing. A certain number of followers of the cultural revolution of May '68 have found the beginnings of a response to their aspirations in the encounter with Eastern traditions, especially with those like the practice of yoga that offered them a cultivation of energy different from the one in which they had been educated.

But Westerners are accustomed to making their energy dependent on ideas or representations. And they have not always known what to do with the energy that they discovered through the practice of yoga, other than to expend it, which did not truly satisfy their aspirations. In fact, they wanted new values and not a lack of values. Nirvana seems to Westerners more like a nihilist solution in the worst sense of the term than like an ideal for their journey. Moreover, the majority of them received a Christian education: they belong to a tradition in which what determines many behaviors is love, unless it is its opposite, hatred. These feelings are largely absent from Eastern teachings, at least as they are received in the West. Even if the importance of relation is stressed by these teachings, it is not imbued with the affective experience and the ideal of the Western tradition. Rather, it is a matter of a strategy in the service of training, of a therapeutic aid, or even of a compassion that is sincere but in which detachment is much more present than it is in the love or friendship of the West. Having become practitioners in a tradition quite different from their own, Westerners are happy to be in better shape, but few of them have found in this cultural values to which to devote themselves and to share in their daily existence.

Practitioners who earn their living by teaching yoga or a similar art have become fervent promoters of European nihilism and/or they are a bit lost, a bit nostalgic, and they do not know how to reconcile their past cultural belonging with their present choice. Without asking too many questions, some accommodate themselves to their practice of yoga and a Christian affiliation. However, things are not so simple. No doubt a cultivation of breath, a practice of concentration and meditation can sustain and enrich a Christian faith and furnish us with a perspective on it. But to which words or images of this tradition can persons who practice yoga remain faithful? Does distance from their Christian education not force them to modify their point of view on it? Does this distance not also lead them to wonder whether or not it is feasible to clear pathways, to become bridges themselves, between the traditions?

This is one of the tasks that we must assume in a multicultural epoch like our own. But are most of the adherents of Eastern traditions, especially of yoga, aware of the responsibility that is incumbent upon them? Do they not content themselves with going from one allegiance to another without worrying about identifying which elements of these traditions might contribute to the elaboration of a present and future culture that would be helpful for their own becoming as well as that of all humanity? In other words, must approaching another culture, such as that of yoga, be for a Westerner a mere survival strategy that is useful to feed or even accelerate the decline of the West and of humankind more generally? Or must it instead represent the search for a path toward an accomplishment of humanity, of which each culture reveals an aspect that has to be discovered and explored with a view toward the construction of a universal culture of which neither the modalities nor the forms can be anticipated?

What seems obvious is that, in order to elaborate a global culture without submitting one tradition to another, we must start again from the real that represents the existing world and humanity itself. It is from the respect for values that are universally necessary for our planet and those who live on it that we most work toward building a culture that is shareable by all humans and, more generally, all living beings who populate the earth. These values first of all concern life itself, its safeguarding and its development, its specificity in accordance with the kingdoms and species, and the fecundity of existence and exchange in diversity. To do no harm requires, above all, that we make life, and its maintenance and growth, possible for each and every living being. This implies personal and political choices in which natural energy is never sacrificed to an artificial energy that is useful only for the profit of some. The use of technique must remain subordinate to the requirements of life and not contribute to its destruction, as is too often the case. It is an entire worldview and a way of governing it that have to be rethought. And the remarks, heard too frequently today, about the choice between saving jobs in industry or saving the planet and its inhabitants testify to an incapacity for innovation, an incapacity to invent an economy in the service of life itself instead of acting to its detriment. They demonstrate a resistance that often goes hand-in-hand with resistance to the affirmation that the difference between the sexes is one of the essential universal values to be preserved and cultivated in our time. Besides the fact that this difference represents the condition for the survival of humanity, it also brings to the latter the most important source of natural energy, an energy that is useful to both social and individual vitality because sexual attraction compels each individual to transcend him- or herself, to go beyond the self, toward an other.

To be sure, belonging to a gender still lacks an appropriate culture and cultivation even though it is at the origin of many cultural products. Humanity has given too little thought to the fact that sexuate identity does not confine itself to sexual attraction, strictly speaking. The latter is extremely important, but being a man or being a woman means belonging to a different relational world that is determined by a different relation to the origin, a different relation to oneself, to the other, and to the world. Such a difference results from a different relation to the mother, to generation itself, and from a specific bodily morphology. The importance of this difference for an individual and collective culture is still unrecognized, as much in the Western tradition as in that of the yoga that I practice. It represents, however, a resource shareable by all cultures beyond any imperialist imposition of values already constructed by one or the other of these cultures.

It is the confinement of women to private property, and the assimilation of the family home to a place reserved for a natural life still deprived of appropriate cultivation, that have obscured the value of the difference between the sexes for the construction of a civil and cultural community, especially at the global level. Evoking the exhaustion of natural resources occurs in many political and economic discourses in our epoch. Unfortunately, they seldom allude to the natural reserves of the human being itself. It would be advisable to be concerned above all about these reserves— especially in terms of the environment, food, and difference between the sexes—in order to prepare a possible future for humanity, a future at once more concerned with human dignity and also more equitable, peaceful, and happy.

Myths and History

TOO OFTEN WE STILL imagine that the diversity of cultures is irreducible and that it is impossible to build bridges between one culture and another. It is even in accordance with the assertions, not to say with the ideology, of certain circles to claim that the difference between cultures is more irreducible than that between the sexes. And yet the latter concerns a natural belonging, while the former concerns a difference of construction starting from natural givens. Certainly differences other than the difference between the sexes exist in these natural givens, such as the original geographical location of a natural or cultural identity. But in all the places in the world, the human species is composed of men and women who have to come to terms with the sexuate morphology of the body and what this implies, with sexual attraction and sexuate relations, with procreation. There are thus constants at work in all races and cultures, even if the manner of treating them varies to some extent from one culture to another.

Most anthropologists pay too little attention to this dimension of human identity and thus they deprive themselves of a crucial key for deciphering the cultural phenomena that appear before them. Their interpretations start from the summit of a cultural construction instead of from a reflection on its foundation, which is in fact universal.

But each human and each tradition needs a passage to an Absolute in order to establish their territories. And it is the modalities of this passage to the absolute that vary and mask the real from which they start. These modalities differ according to the space in which they originate and even more so according to time. They testify to the evolution of humanity and the necessities relative to each stage of its evolution.

Alas, few cultures, and indeed few individuals, assume the relative nature of their absolute—which maintains oppositions and conflicts that are detrimental to the becoming of humanity. Few traditions and individuals are able to step back and put into perspective the way they have elaborated their relation to the absolute. This is understandable: they have made this absolute the keystone of an individual or social construction, the origin of which they have forgotten. One could even say: the keystone of a cultural edification built in order to maintain the oblivion of the origin. It seems that this happens more and more the further one goes along in the evolution of humanity, especially from the time when a culture develops by itself with neither reference nor return to its natural beginning and determination. Thus, for example, the privileging of the neuter ends in the oblivion of the sexuate character of life, of the unfolding of history, its existence, and its necessities—which stops any evolution for humanity.

For a history built by starting from the real, there has been progressively substituted a history built starting from the repression, the negation, or only a partial aspect of the real—a history elaborated by a so-called neuter or asexuate individual, which is in fact masculine, obedient only to the requirements or needs of this individual to liberate himself from the natural or maternal world. The real origin of this subject and of humanity has been sent back to prehistory, to the "dark continent" where, according to Freud, the mystery of feminine identity and desires would be concealed. From this epoch, works of art and myths would remain that still tell us about our sexuate identity and about the manner in which humans as well as gods lived and even shared it.

These myths are not always the same even though they present permanent features related to the question of the origin of the world and of humanity as well as to the relations, particularly amorous but also social, between the sexes. The myths specific to each human group represent a set of beliefs that bind the group together through truths regarding its origin and its ancestors, but also the heroes or gods that embody certain laws or ideals acting as models to be respected, feared, or imitated. The body of myths serves as a sort of reference to an absolute that ensures the cohesion of the group. Not respecting it amounts to violating the code that unites the group, to transgressing the cultural boundaries of its territory.

The representations of the absolute are therefore partially relative because they correspond to what defines the identity of one human group in relation to another. One could even say that the absolute is in some way in the service of the relative, even if it is not imagined as such.

Entry into history would be determined by the use of a writing that allows the events or facts pertaining to the evolution of humanity to be recorded and remembered. Writing is nonfigurative in most cultures, and the codes that it obeys are often abstract with respect to the real: they no longer express the real as it is, and they are no longer universal either. Paradoxically, at the very moment when humanity discovers writing in order to recall real facts, it is compelled to make reference to an unrepresentable truth of which written proofs could give only a partial account. The Absolute accompanying the use of writing escapes the popular imagination, which is from then on constrained to submit to the discourse of clerics, philosophers, or scientists in order to learn something about it. The energy that each one needs to project onto an Absolute in order to make one's way through existence remains suspended in the interpretation of the Absolute given by the clerics in a specific time and place in History. The faithful must then make their energy dependent on an Absolute that they themselves do not perceive and the Truth of which would truly be revealed to them only after death.

However, in the perception of the Absolute resulting from the use of a nonfigurative writing, there enter mythical elements that transform into the Absolute that which is lived as such only in a particular place and a particular epoch of history. But neither the popular imagination nor even that of most clerics is any longer able to assess the relative character of this Absolute. Indeed, notably and not by chance, what is most vital about human energy—that is, sexual desire—has been paralyzed by blind faith in a disembodied Absolute in which the subject perceives no value here and now for his or her human flourishing.

There remains the historic possibility of a divine made man—or, more generally, the possibility of a becoming-divine for the human itself. No longer is this a projection onto the gods or God of a human ideal, rather it corresponds to the incarnation in the human itself of the divine dimension hitherto deferred into the beyond. This stage of human evolution could open an epoch of nonconflictual coexistence between diverse elaborations of the Absolute—according to epochs, places, generations, sexes. We would be confronted then with another task in relation to the Absolute. The matter would no longer be one of our submission to something or to someone inaccessible in our earthly existence—laying down the law to us without our being allowed to verify its truth—but of our being able to divinize ourselves without pretending, for all that, to succeed in corresponding to a single and unique Absolute. Such a divinization would therefore mean the fulfillment of humanity by each one in a noncompetitive collaboration with everyone else. Each culture, each generation, each sex would contribute to the realization of the human and would exchange with the other starting from the path taken, the journey accomplished, the transformation of energy carried out. The progress of each one would be useful to everyone instead of being capitalized on in favor of a specific Absolute, which puts the different paths of humanity into conflict.

"Pure utopia!" some will object. But without this utopia will there be a future for humanity? Do we not have to discover a new mode of accomplishing humanity that permits the coexistence, in respect for their differences, of humans henceforth more adult and less dependent upon ideal models particular to their traditions? Figures such as Buddha on the one hand and Jesus on the other: do they not foreshadow, although in a way that is still partial or partially interpreted, a possible becoming for humanity? Could not a culture of breath, a culture of love, serve as the basis for the development of a global human community without the submission of one culture to another? And the bridge between East and West, this bridge that we must build and that we must be: does it not demand that we unite, in us and between us, the transformation of breath and of vital instincts within a culture of spiritual and relational energy that enables us to enter into another epoch of human evolution instead of contributing to the decline of humanity? An epoch that will discover, beyond the opposition between silence and speech that distinguishes the Eastern from the Western path, a mode of communicating in which gesture will play a bigger role. And in which art—especially the work of art that the living being can become—will be a way of entering into relation with the other, thereby facilitating an exchange cultivated between different human beings who appear to one another in their entirety: body, heart, breath, listening, speech, and thought, with a view toward a sharing capable of engendering a new humanity.

{ II }

The Mystery of Mary

To Introduce the Mystery of Mary

TRANSLATED BY LUCE IRIGARAY
AND ANTONIA PONT

AS AMERICAN PUBLISHERS are not (yet?) in favor of the publication of small books, I therefore proposed to add to *A New Culture of Energy* another short text, *The Mystery of Mary*. Even if this text has already been published separately in some languages, it is appropriate to gather the two texts in the same volume because my interpretation of the figure of Mary would not have been possible without my having done yoga for more than forty years and my approach to Eastern cultures, in particular those which relate to yoga. Indeed, my reading of the figure of Mary focuses on breathing. The virginity of Mary is interpreted as a capability to preserve the artlessness and the receptiveness of an autonomous breathing and the event of the Annunciation as the awakening of a higher breath, in order that Mary could welcome the other as other, even in herself, without losing her maidenhood. The positive meaning of the silence of Mary is assessed in the light of Eastern cultures, which consider keeping silent to be the end of the path toward a gathering with oneself—as a Buddha shows. Mary is also viewed as a figure of wisdom, who is compared with feminine figures of other traditions, among others that of Parvati, the partner of the god Siva who is able to transform the fire of the god into a source of creation instead of a cause of destruction, unlike his other partner, Kali.

In my view, Mary incarnates feminine values which have more, or still, to do with an Eastern tradition that Western culture has mistakenly forgotten, and even repressed. Gathering together *A New Culture of Energy* and *The Mystery of Mary* in the same volume can thus contribute to the two texts shedding light on one another, and more generally to Eastern and Western culture shedding light to one another. And this represents a task which is incumbent on us in this age.

Prologue

OF MARY, we know almost nothing. The Gospels give us only a few rather anecdotal words on her, which tell us little about her and her relationship with the divine. In religious services today, Mary is barely present. For example, in my parish, at Christmas time, she is generally evoked only during the mass reserved for children. The feasts devoted to Mary according to the calendar—for instance, the supposed date of her birthday (September 8), that of the Annunciation (March 25), and that of the Assumption (August 15)—are hardly ever celebrated. What is more, in the church of my quarter, the statue that represents Mary as the mother of God was recently moved—for greater convenience, they explained—from a main chapel situated behind the choir to a secondary altar, where it is henceforth among other saints. Other representations of Mary—those corresponding to her appearances at Lourdes or at Fatima—are grouped together in a sort of chapel at the back of the church with other highly venerated saints, such as Saint Anthony or Saint Rita.

And yet Mary marks the entrance into the Christian era. Without her, the Good News of Christianity would simply not exist. She is the necessary condition for Incarnation, the first mediation, the first mediator, between divinity and humanity, between God and humans, in order that a possible redemption of the world could happen.

Moreover, popular fervor is not mistaken. It trustingly turns toward Mary, builds or dedicates numerous sanctuaries to her, flocks in pilgrimages devoted to her. It sings Mary's praises or implores her, including in literature and popular song, even when it gives up more official places and forms of worship. Could all that be a mere naivete, a remainder of paganism, an inability to attain to a truly spiritual level? Rather, would it not be a question of a mystery revealed to children, to the humble, to the poor in spirit, to pure hearts, to those who cry and hunger for justice? Mystery of the part of woman in our redemption, a part that remains almost unknown to a learned Western theology, whose logic, predominantly masculine, has been elaborated to the detriment of our incarnation. Mystery about which such a theology can say nothing appropriate unless, sometimes, in the form of reverence, of prayers or songs of praise, and also of aporia in its discourse.

Divine from Birth

THE DIVINE IS LINKED with air, with breath. The one who is designated by the name of God in our tradition creates with his breath, and those who enjoy spiritual powers have a relationship with air, with wind, with the source and movement of life. By contrast the diabolical likes confinement, fears drafts, and can adapt to fire but not to air. Mimic of the living, the diabolical does not breathe, or no longer breathes: it steals air from others, from the world.

In a way, we are divine from birth, and it is a lack of cultivation of our breathing that leads us to lose our divinity. The episode of original sin, as told in Genesis, may be interpreted in this sense. Instead of cultivating their vital breathing, of transforming it little by little into love, into listening and speech, into thought, woman and man wanted to eat the forbidden fruit in order to acquire a knowledge that was not theirs, of which they were not capable. A culture of breathing brings awakening, a knowledge of the divine in ourselves, whereas leaving ourselves in order to appropriate the knowledge of the other leads to a forgetting of the source of the divine and makes us diabolical.

If woman is imagined to be the first one guilty of original sin, it is probably because she has a privileged relation to breath. Feminine breath remains both more linked to the life of the universe and more interior; it joins, without rupture, the most subtle aspects of the cosmos and of the body to what is most spiritual in the soul. Woman must not separate from nature in order to humanize it, to spiritualize it. If she remains faithful to herself, she can render nature divine or redeem it by unceasingly uniting earth and heaven, thanks to a transformation of matter through breath, beginning with a spiritualization of her own breath. Remaining more in communion with the universe, whose air nourishes and purifies the breath, woman is also more capable of keeping her breath in herself so that she can share it with the other in love or in pregnancy and in motherhood. More cut off from the natural world, man mostly uses his breath for doing, producing, or creating outside himself.

Because she has a privileged relation to breath, the divine is more fully present in the little girl. This explains why certain traditions have chosen a small or an adolescent girl to embody the divinity, whereas, for the masculine, it is rather an old man who fulfils this role, particularly in the Judeo-Christian tradition. It would not be at the same age that woman and man could lead to blossoming the divine in themselves. And it is to an adolescent girl, still a virgin, that the task of redeeming humanity and bringing it back to its divine dimension has been entrusted in our tradition.

The Event of the Annunciation

STILL CARNALLY a virgin, Mary retains the fullness of the feminine identity of a little girl. She is already autonomous with respect to her genealogy, especially with respect to her mother, and her flesh, like her breathing, is not yet intimately mingled with those of another human being. Mary is still in communion with herself and with the universe through her breathing. She is adolescent, already pubescent, but she still breathes as a girl, or almost so. Her body begins to be moved and to retain breathing in parts of her that are less in relation with the whole. It is at this moment that the angel intervenes.

Before her breathing becomes at the service of a merely natural procreation, Mary is called by an angel, the messenger or the embodiment of the divine breath, to awaken, as a woman, to a breathing that is not merely vital but also spiritual. The angel shares breath with her, and addresses words to her to which she listens and responds. Thus, the announcement of the conception of a child does not limit itself to an emotion or to a material or physical sharing. It is an exchange of words.

The very rich iconography of the Annunciation shows that the scene focuses, with regard to the body of Mary, at the level of the sternum, that is, at the level of the bone thanks to which the first seven ribs, at the bottom, are articulated with the two clavicles, at the top. It is here that Mary often holds her crossed hands, as if she wants to protect a treasure, the one which results from the transformation of her vital breathing into a spiritually shareable amorous breathing. In certain icons, the baby Jesus is also represented in this place.

The Judeo-Christian tradition does not tell us of divine couples who exist, however, in other traditions. Perhaps such couples could happen in a third age, that of the Holy Spirit, after the age of creation, of original sin, and the redemption of humanity. The age when an awakening and a cultivation of breathing would allow a sharing between those who love each other to be not only carnal, but also spiritual.

This has not yet occurred at the moment of the Annunciation. It was not yet then a question of union between divine spouses, such as the one evoked at the end of the Apocalypse of John. Nor is it simply a matter of gods who descend from the heavens in order to love a mortal woman and to make her pregnant, more often than not with a male child, a future mediator between men and gods—as is the case in Greek mythology.

We know almost nothing about the love life of Mary, save that she was engaged to a man named Joseph, and thus had not opted for chastity, at least on the physical plane. Besides, it is not at the level of a natural procreation that the angel awakens her but rather at the level of a higher breathing, a breathing animated by love and by words permitting communication, indeed communion, between two different beings. God does not leave word, his word, in Mary in order that it germinate there as if in a fertile earth, almost without her knowing it and independently of her will. God exchanges words with Mary, asking her to accept him coming to live with her, in her.

At that time, the God of Israel was without a dwelling and his existence was somehow in peril, torn in conflicts and wars between men or peoples who wanted in one way or another to appropriate his power, his truth, his word. Instead of living, blossoming, and sharing their humanity, the first couple of Genesis aspired to situate themselves immediately at a mental level of which man and woman were not capable and which plunged them into suffering and expelled them from the Garden of Eden, which was their living place. The divine knowledge, which they had attempted to appropriate, without first attending to being humans, became a source of suffering for each of them and of discord between the two.

The divine truth also became lost in multiple and partial interpretations that were debated between men in more or less warlike ways. Man, on the one hand, and the truth of the word, on the other, moved more and more away from one another. It was necessary that the word become incarnate in order that unity should be recovered as well as a truth that humanity might again perceive as a horizon of transcendence. However, such an incarnation required a virginity that was not only natural but also spiritual, one that would be capable of listening to and welcoming such a word.

Instead of humanity being created solely from earth, water, and divine breath, the word will henceforth intervene in human begetting. The word needs to become flesh in order to remain alive, animated by breath, and humanity needs the word in order to pursue its becoming between natural belonging and spiritual belonging, the latter little by little transforming, transfiguring the former.

Woman left herself, abandoned her own breath in order to appropriate divine knowledge, according to Genesis, and the same thing happened when she went in search of her beloved, according to the Song of Songs. The announcement of the angel brought her back again to her breath so that she could ensure the redemption of humanity. But this breath from then on joins with the word. It is called by the angel in the place where it nourishes the heart, the spiritual certainty, and the word—according to the definition of the centers, or chakras, that unite physical and psychic energy in certain Eastern traditions.

The Genesis tells us that the woman's breath was born, at least in part, from that of man. However, it is from the breath of a woman that the breath of man will henceforth arise to attain the redemption of the world.

A child always depends for its development on the mother's breathing: the oxygen the child needs is provided by the mother's blood. The event of the Annunciation transforms this natural phenomenon into a spiritual one. This natural phenomenon is already, to a certain degree, spiritual, but without this being said and consecrated by an other, in the Gospel, by a messenger of God. The angel draws the attention of Mary to the fact that she cannot give birth to a divine child, and in particular to a son, without committing herself to being faithful to the virginity of her breathing: that is, without preserving a reserve of breath, of soul capable of welcoming and of sharing with an other, respecting this other as different while also being true to her own spiritual life. Something that requires Mary to have a personal bond to the divine, a bond unmediated by man, and to remain faithful to it. The event of the Annunciation establishes or celebrates this bond between Mary and God—independently of her people, of her genealogy, of the man to whom she was engaged, and even independently of her future child.

The Virginity of Mary

TOO OFTEN, the virginity of Mary is spoken of in terms that are contemptuous of her, of all women, and of our religious tradition itself. God, like an absolute patriarch, would in a way have made use of the adolescent Mary to father himself a son without any amorous relations with her, either at the corporeal or at the spiritual level. God would have mysteriously engendered a son in Mary through the mediation of the Spirit, the divine figure representing the love between Father and Son in the Christian Trinity. It is from such a love that Mary would have conceived, without herself participating carnally or spiritually in this conception. In current words, one could say that Mary agreed to carry a child that was not really hers.

Such an interpretation of Incarnation still undermines the very foundations of Christianity. Indeed, what could a divine incarnation mean if this presupposes no carnal or spiritual intervention from the woman in giving birth to God becoming man? This hypothesis is offensive, even for God of our tradition. He would have behaved like the most domineering of overlords, exercising a "Lords First Night" toward the fiancée of Joseph.

It is difficult to admit that the fecundity of the Christian message could take root in such a problematic act, whatever may be the various metaphors with which one adorns it. Now still today, and perhaps more than ever, eminent theologians, otherwise very open to ecumenical perspectives, support such an interpretation of Jesus' birth. This interpretation would be needed in order to keep human and divine nature separate, they argue in terms more Platonic than Christian.

But if certain theologians, of yesterday or today, have wondered, in a very naturalistic and somewhat perversely indiscreet way, about the physiological hymen of Mary, which of them has been concerned by the spiritual role of Mary in the conception of Jesus and the redemption of humanity? And yet this redemption cannot happen without the spiritual participation of Mary. If the 'yes' of Mary, during the event of the Annunciation, is a mere assent of a slave to the caprice of a patriarch, the time of Incarnation, as the redemption of the world, cannot exist. And, no doubt, this era has not yet fully happened, and we still go no further than a separation between body and spirit, which prevents us from taking an active part in our own becoming divine and the becoming divine of the universe in which we live.

This is especially the case for women, who are kept by the interpretation of their role in Incarnation in total dependence upon the goodwill of man, who is presumed to be more divine by nature than them and is presupposed to remain the mediator between them and God. Man, whose seed—be it simple sperm or word—would be what is capable of begetting thanks to a feminine ground whose only properties would be to be welcoming, fecund, and nourishing. These properties are today still valorized and praised as peculiar to woman because they permit her integration into a community, be it ecclesiastic or other, where she is at the service of her lord(s) and master(s). This gives woman no chance of preserving her spiritual virginity for a natural or a spiritual giving birth.

In order to render the mystery of Incarnation credible and respectable, the virginity of Mary—like that of any woman—must correspond to her ability to keep her breath autonomous and partly available for the advent of a not yet come to pass future and the encounter with an other respected in their transcendence. This implies that Mary be not merely at the disposal of a lord, even if divine, but be instead capable of maintaining herself in order to ensure her own spiritual becoming and a spiritual exchange with the other, in particular with the different other—be this other a father, an amorous partner, or a son.

Preserving one's virginity requires an aptitude for contemplation and for intimacy with oneself. The little that we know, or that has been imagined, about Mary bears witness to the significance of such attitudes in all that concerns her.

The Silence of Mary

IN WESTERN CULTURE, to speak is more valued than keeping silent. The one who speaks demonstrates one's capacities, whereas the one, especially she, who remains silent admits their powerlessness or submission. The meaning of speaking in relation to silence is the opposite in certain traditions, for example, Eastern ones. For a philosopher like Hegel, the end of our journey would correspond to a gathering of all the possible discourses, and our God is the one who holds the key to the truth of the word. On the contrary, Buddha is the sage capable of reaching silence. In one case, we must aim at speaking, in the other at silence. Silence, then, does not signify an absence of something, especially an absence of words, but rather the achievement of oneself, the completion of a perfect interiority. Some representations of Buddha show the realization of such a silence leading to a serene contemplation of his whole being. Buddha belongs to a culture less masculine than our own, in which doing, creating, or speaking outside oneself is appreciated in relation to a more internal work and path.

The silence of Mary is often interpreted in a negative manner, particularly by women. This negative judgment is inspired by Western values that are predominantly masculine. The silence of Mary may be understood in another way. It can signify a means of preserving an

intimacy with oneself, a self-affection, in order not to get lost, notably in a discourse that is not one's own.

The silence that goes with the lips that touch one another is not
necessarily negative but may represent, on the contrary, a special
place for the preservation of one's self through a re-touching, of the
borders of our body marking the threshold between the inside and
the outside, the mucous membranes and the skin. Bringing one's lips
together—as bringing one's hands, and also one's eyelids together—
is a means of gathering with one's self, of reuniting the two parts of
oneself in order to gather with oneself and to dwell in, or to return
to, oneself.

To experience this communing with our self through the two
parts of ourselves touching one another is necessary for our being
able to live an affect in the relations with the other without losing
ourselves. It is essential to depart from and to return to the union
of the two that we are before we become capable of living a relation
between two with an other who is different. Without this self-affection, this gathering with ourselves, we continually run the risk of
confusing the other with a part of ourselves, or of confusing ourselves, at least in part, with the other.

In Greek mythology, we can observe a negative evolution in the
position of the lips in sculptures of the young goddess Kore between
the moment when she is an adolescent virgin and the moment after
she has been taken away from her mother and married by force to
the god of the underworld, Hades. Before the rape by Hades her
lips are harmoniously closed, touching one another; then they are
deformed and, finally, the mouth no longer closes completely, the
lips remaining open. Kore-Persephone has lost the intimacy with
herself, the possibility of returning to herself, of dwelling in herself
after her rape by the god of the underworld.

The relevance of closing the lips for keeping an intimacy with
oneself also explains the rejection reaction of the young Dora when
Mr. K attempts to kiss her while they are watching a procession.
Freud interprets such a gesture as a neurotic symptom, whereas it

appears to me as a quite justified and sane wish to preserve an intimacy with oneself—especially during a religious event—from a
man who wants to compel the young girl to love him by alleging that
she desires him without admitting it. Which corresponds to a way
of forcing her, of raping her, not only at a physical level but also at a
psychological and spiritual level.

The importance of keeping the lips closed, touching one another,
is also taught to us through the sacred universal syllable *om*. In this
syllable, the final letter, *m*, whose pronunciation requires us to shut
again the lips, is supposed to safeguard what has not yet appeared.
And this letter is said to correspond to the color black.

Therefore, the silence of Mary is not necessarily an absence
of words, but it can be a reserve of future words or events whose
appearing did not yet occur. Mary—like every woman?—would be
the one who carries in her the mystery of what did not yet happen,
beyond all that has already appeared. This would be true not only
at the level of a natural but also of a spiritual giving birth. Bringing a divine child into the world signifies bringing into the world a
new epoch of humanity's history. And it is a woman who is asked to
accomplish such a task by the one to whom we give the name God.

This interpretation is possible, and it entrusts woman with a decisive part in the incarnation of the divine on earth. Many women, in
our tradition, are incapable of recognizing that they have a privileged
task to take on for the coming of the divine into the world. The truly
masculine character of our culture prevents them from valuing their
foundational role in the spiritual becoming of humanity, a role that
they neglect, and even scorn, in comparison with the more social
and visible ecclesiastical responsibilities which are rather incumbent
upon men.

Visible and Invisible

IF MARY IS in a certain sense visible, her works to a great extent are not visible. Certainly, she gives birth to Jesus, but the way she carries this out remains secret. For example, the account of Genesis describes the creation of man as the result of God's sending out his breath into matter, but who tells us that Mary shares her breath with the fetus in order to give birth to a child? The Annunciation indicates that the angel awakens the breath of Mary at a higher level. However, no text or even image—except perhaps certain icons?—reveals to us that Jesus needed the breath of Mary to come into the world. He would have been mysteriously conceived by the word of God, but about the invisible sharing of breath between Mary and Jesus silence is kept. She ought to have been a mere receptacle, a mere vehicle and food for begetting the son of God. Now, the participation of Mary in this begetting is far more secretly spiritual than is said.

The sexuate identity of Jesus is also different from that of Mary. To respect the other as other, to give this other hospitality and life, not only in one's country or in one's home but in oneself, requires an ability to transcend oneself that Mary shows. It is not only the absolute—understood in a somehow quantitative sense—transcendence of God who takes part in bringing the divine child into the world, it is also the corporeal and psychic work that is needed by the gestation of a being different from oneself. For a woman, accepting the irreducible difference between herself and the one she conceives, the one she carries, is not limited to a mere natural work. This requires opening to a transcendence in relation to herself, a transcendence that is no longer that of a God shareable between a mother and a child but corresponds to the irreducible alterity of the other. The ethical gesture of Mary, as a woman, is not only to respect the life of the other but also to give birth to an other who is naturally and spiritually different from her. Through this gesture, when it is voluntarily and freely assumed—as it is by Mary, according to the Bible—the woman has already overcome the natural identity to which our culture, including Christian theology, has too often reduced her. She testifies to an aptitude for respecting the transcendence of the other, something of which few men are effectively capable. This gesture remains, however, to a great extent, invisible. Nevertheless, the simple sight of a woman carrying a son in her arms inspires consideration for her transcending herself that such a begetting asks of a woman. A behavior of which not all women are capable, whence some gestures of appropriation or rejection which mean the difficulty, for a mother, in completely respecting her son as different from her. But all the discourses about the necessary intervention of the father to separate the mother-nature from the child forget how a woman already transcended herself in order to accomplish such a giving birth. The intervention of the angel, addressing the higher breath of Mary and exchanging words with her, would appear more suitable for assisting Mary in her invisible effort to give life, both natural and spiritual, to the one who is transcendent to her.

Emphasizing the mother in Mary—as is generally the case in order to give value to a woman—certainly results from the preeminence of the visible over the invisible in our tradition. This one, however, imagines God as totally invisible to man, at least from a certain epoch onward. What our tradition ignores is the presence of the invisible in the visible, an aspect connected with the transformation of matter itself, a matter, then, that is not subjected to the opposition between matter and spirit, body and soul. Certainly, some episodes in the life of Jesus, as in that of Buddha, allude to a transmutation of matter: for example, the transfiguration of Jesus or the aura emanating from Buddha. With regard to Jesus, the resurrection of the body could also be interpreted in this way. And for Mary, the fact that she can "ascend to heaven" without having to pass through death and resurrection. But the work of transmutation of matter that she achieves in herself in order to transform her vital breath into a spiritual breath, in order to safeguard her virginity even in giving birth, as well as to respect the other as other while remaining faithful to herself, is not seen. Unless we change our way of looking, unless we learn to contemplate the invisible in the visible instead of wanting to seize the other in a defined form, thereby running the risk of reducing her or him to a mere appearing.

Touched by Grace

IN THE WESTERN TRADITION, sensory perceptions are considered to be inferior to mental activity and must be subordinated to it. Often, moreover, we express what we perceive through abstract generic words that have already removed their living qualities, as much from the object of our perception as from our perceptions themselves. We look at a tree, we listen to music, we appreciate a meal or a smell, without stopping to contemplate a birch, enjoy an impromptu of Schubert, savor a peach, or breathe in the scent of a forest of pines under the summer sun or after rain. Now, lingering on perceiving a living reality, and on its sensory qualities, instead of abstractly evoking it through a word, can help us to be more present at what surrounds us or at ourselves. It can also awaken us to a way of perceiving that is more attentive, respectful, and loving. Furthermore, if I linger in perceiving a living being, I will note that something of this being will never be completely perceptible to me through my senses. To look at a daisy or a rose will never render visible to me the sap that keeps the flower alive, a sap starting from which this flower can appear to me without my ever being able to appropriate it. By respecting the invisible of the flower, my perception acquires a more global dimension, a more contemplative quality—and it becomes insensibly spiritual.

This is even more true when it is the question of another human, especially a human who is different from me. By lingering on perceiving him or her at a sensible level—on looking, on listening to their voice, on touching—while respecting their otherness—that is to say, as him or her being partly invisible, inaudible, untouchable by me—I go from a mere physical perception to a spiritual perception of the other. This development allows us to share love without submission or appropriation of the one by the other.

A culture of our sensory perceptions ought to have a crucial part in a tradition of incarnation, and it ought to lead us little by little to the perception of a sensible, incarnated transcendence. Our culture, including Christian culture, still considers to be transcendent that which escapes our sensory perceptions, which is disembodied. This corresponds to submitting the Christian message to a philosophical logic extraneous to it, a logic defined, for the most part, by men, notably in order to emancipate themselves from their natural or maternal origin, without their solving the question of the spiritual becoming of their sensible and bodily belonging and relations.

To subject Jesus, and before him, Mary, to such a philosophical perspective amounts to being unaware of the meaning of divine incarnation for our human evolution. However, the texts teach us the importance of sensory perceptions for the Good News of the Gospels. Mary pays attention to her environment and to others in their natural and spiritual existence. Mary is in no way lost in discourses or abstractly ideal behaviors that would exile her from her terrestrial life. Unlike Eve, Mary is so faithfully and humbly terrestrial that most of our Western theological interpretations reduce her to a mere vehicle of the divine instead of recognizing her as the first divine figure of the time of Incarnation. Artists, however, have not been mistaken, at least not those who have endeavored to transpose into diverse kinds of images, into icons, into music, and even into poetical words, what they experienced about the presence of Mary. Perhaps no subject has inspired artists more than this woman so absent from theology. And, no doubt, art has been the most faithful means of passing on the Christian message.

Jesus himself bears witness to the importance of sensory perceptions in his relations with the world and, above all, with others. It is almost always in the middle of nature that he meets his disciples and speaks with them, nature with which he shows a profound intimacy throughout his life and even at the time of his death. The language of Jesus is more poetic than abstractly philosophical. He cares about the needs, and even the desires, of those who come to meet him, who welcome him in their homes, who love him. He often cures the ills by touching, including through his words, or has recourse to partially material and terrestrial means—earth or water—to treat them. He also appeals to the inner life, to the trust, of the one who searches for him in order to be in communion with him or her and this way cures or purifies them of their pains.

Grace, including that of the Annunciation, happens thanks to a touching, and not through the mediation of an abstract language that speaks solely to the mind and resorts to more or less arbitrary codes. The mystery of divine incarnation cannot be fulfilled without the mediation of touch, including a sensible, a carnal touch. The men, and mainly the women, who have refused the abstract, ritual, and coded nature of the transmission of the Christian message, that is the mystics, have revived the importance of touch, including the tactile nature of grace, in this tradition. Nevertheless, this has too often involved paroxysms or excessive sufferings to cross back over all that had exiled them from their innocent and virginal relations with touch.

Would not a culture of touch, as the passage for mediating the reception of grace in us and between us, be a manner of bearing witness to our trust and faithfulness toward the mystery of Incarnation, into what we are initiated by the Annunciation?

A Figure of Wisdom

IF MARY USHERS us into the Christian era, she is not really recognized in Christianity, except as a mother somewhat mysteriously co-engendering the baby Jesus, future redeemer of the world. Mary belongs to a pantheon of mother-goddesses whom we find in all traditions.

Unlike most of these mythical figures, Mary does not arouse ambivalence. She is the all-good, all-pure mother from whom nothing is to be feared. This bestows on her an almost unique status among representations of the mother-goddesses. Certainly, one might compare her to certain Greek goddesses—for example, Demeter. But Demeter does not show the irreproachable purity, the unfailing goodness and faithfulness of Mary. Furthermore, in the myths concerning Demeter, it is the relation to the fecundity of the earth that is stressed and not the spiritual character of the breath, especially in giving birth.

If Mary is removed from her merely maternal role, if she is considered to be first a woman, one might compare her to one of the feminine partners of the Indian god, Shiva, the god who corresponds to our era. Of Shiva one says that he can lead the world toward its destruction or to its salvation, according to whether his partner is Kali, generally represented as black, or Parvati, whose color is instead white. Kali is the one who heightens the fire of Shiva's passion, whereas Parvati tempers and soothes it, notably through love. Like Mary, Parvati corresponds to the pure, in a sense the virginal, nature of the god, contributing toward making of his fire a source of creation or regeneration rather than of destruction. If Parvati is called the lady of the mountain, that is, of a place where the air is subtle, pure, and fresh, it is also generally on a hill that Mary appears. There are thus some affinities between the two feminine figures, which can allow us to approach and better interpret certain universal paradigms of the divine dimension. For example, it can help us not to imagine or believe too quickly that the virginity of Mary signifies a mere carnal abstinence instead of an ability to transform or transmute flesh itself. We would be risking, then, confusing the virginity of Mary with the behavior without moderation of Eve with regard to the journey of humanity toward its becoming divine, or even submitting it to masculine models for which a spiritual sharing of flesh seems apparently to be still unknown.

In reality, Mary appears as a woman who represents and safeguards the traditions of wisdom in a universe of men, where fire is often predominant and indeed destructive. She is the one who even succeeds in calming the anger of God, in transforming his need or desire for vengeance into compassion, into love. Mary is the mediator between God and humans. She is the one who smiles before their follies—something that also occurs in relation to Jesus, the Gospels tell us—who attempts to tone them down and to intercede on humans' behalf with God to solicit his patience and to obtain his clemency toward the extravagances of men. For Mary, spirit would be less fire than freshness of a breath that rises, becomes more subtle, turned into ether and light.

Such transformation of breath, particularly of the amorous breath, into light that can save from the destructive qualities of fire is almost unknown to us Westerners. And the decisive role that can be played by a woman in such a culture of wisdom remains ignored, and even scorned, by most of us. It is, however, both complex and determining for a vital and spiritual becoming of humanity. It requires us not only to act outside ourselves, which at once uses up our energy and produces a less natural energy that becomes destructive—something in which men, but also machines, excel. A culture of wisdom needs an internal work, a doing but also a letting do and letting be that welcomes, while transforming, what happens in oneself. Women are more capable than men of such behavior, at least when they remain faithful to themselves. And this is essential today for the survival and becoming of humanity.

This internal process of human spiritualization demands humility—a virtue as much discredited as virginity, due to an interpretation that misjudges its real meaning. Humility is that which allows one to remain open and welcoming, but not blindly subjected, toward the world, the other, and grace. It is a critical element of a culture of wisdom and not a mere psychic attitude that shows only docility and subjection in the face of a master.

A Bridge in Time and Space

TRADITIONS OF WISDOM have existed and still exist in certain cultures. They correspond to societies or communities in which women are more present and have more influence on cultural and spiritual life. It is acquaintance with such traditions—notably through doing yoga and approaching cultures linked up to it—that allowed me to perceive something of the person of Mary outside the interpretations of a patriarchal and phallocentric tradition like our own.

My commitment in favor of the liberation of women, and more generally of human liberation, has also led me to read some works about cultures preceding ours and which ours has gradually erased, substituting other values for them. The activity of man; technology; more or less conflictual and warlike competitiveness; quantitative assessment, finally valued in terms of money; exchanges between humans and of humans themselves have little by little supplanted a respect for life and for its growth; a privilege of natural fecundity over artificial creation or fabrication; a more embodied, predominantly artistic language; and a community organization related to the real of genealogy and of the natural environment and not dependent on more or less arbitrary and abstract laws and codes.

A masculine order has gradually prevailed over a feminine order. And it is not a coincidence that the essential aspect of the Christian message has been progressively focused solely on the person of Jesus to the detriment of the figure of Mary and her role as co-redeemer of the world. The separation between the churches of the East and the West has speeded up and established such an evolution. But it is not sure that a reading of the Gospels, henceforth really dependent on Western metaphysics, is truly faithful to the message of Incarnation and to its redemptive function. It sometimes seems that we have fallen back into the mistake of Eve, who wanted to appropriate divine knowledge, rendering man her accomplice in such an enterprise, before even being capable of cultivating her own breath, of making divine her own nature toward a spiritual sharing with the other including at a carnal level.

I am not unaware of the low opinion many Western women—especially intellectuals and feminists—have of Mary. It is not impossible that their judgment is determined by a masculine culture from which they believe to free themselves, though they submit to it, for lack of foreseeing an other. It is true that constructing a new culture is more difficult and demanding than criticizing the one that already exists. And the silence of Mary, unlike the texts of the Gospels, sets nothing and leaves us free to invent a future as we wish. Even then, it is advisable to choose a future that corresponds to a fidelity to ourselves, to a culture of our own energy, and not to a loss of our forces through imitating values that do not suit us or through claims and conflicts.

No doubt, confining Mary to being mother of a son does not encourage women of our times to be interested in her, to wonder about her, because she, then, appears to them as a slave and a support to patriarchal power. However, it does not seem that the person of Mary can be confined to such a function. By gathering together all the passages of the Gospels that evoke her, by contemplating all the representations of her that artists offer to us, by considering all the works of art that she has inspired, all the favors and aids that she has lavished, how could we not wonder about the mystery that Mary represents? A mystery that has not yet told all its secrets, and which will remain always partially a mystery, given the part of touch, of intimacy and invisibility that come into it. A mystery that has been, as requested by our tradition, mistaken for the maternal role of Mary, instead of being situated in her feminine identity—though she continues to appear to the world under such a form.

It is first in Mary as a woman that the mystery, or the mystic dimension, lies and will not be unveiled in our culture and, perhaps, will never be unveiled. For it is part of the integrity of a feminine presence: the embodiment of a mystery that cannot be unveiled. That is not to say, however, that this presence might not be approached in ways other than through our logic and discourses founded on our rationality, when it does not incur only violence and contempt or merely ignorance and forgetting. This presence can be approached, for example, through art, poetic words or song, gestures of contemplation or of self-affection extraneous to narcissistic withdrawal or arrogance, and through a culture of breathing and a practice of concentration that does not stop at any precise object.

This presence can also be sensed thanks to silence—our own and that of Mary—a silence that is a return to, and a peaceful dwelling within, oneself in order to restore or preserve there a fullness from which a future still to happen might germinate and spring. The one that we are still awaiting. That of the embodiment of the divine presence of a woman. A woman capable of being a temporal bridge between the past, the present, and the future, and a spatial bridge between all the cultures of the world, thanks to her spiritual virginity—a safeguarding of a living and free breath, irreducible to anyone or to anything.